JUST ONE
MORE TIME

JUST ONE MORE TIME

THE MIRACLE OF
GEORGIA SOUTHERN FOOTBALL

Jim Halley and **Mark McClellan**

PHOTOGRAPHS BY FRANK FORTUNE

Peachtree Publishers, Ltd.

Published by
Peachtree Publishers, Ltd.
494 Armour Circle, N.E.
Atlanta, Georgia 30324

Manufactured in the United States of America

Design by Paulette L. Lambert

10 9 8 7 6 5 4 3 2 1

Library of Congress Catalog Card Number 87-80969

ISBN 0-934601-24-0

Special thanks to the Georgia Southern College Athletic Department; to Ric Mandes, director of the Division of Institutional Development; and to photographer Frank Fortune for their assistance and support in producing this book.

1/ The Top Of The Mountain

The scene was all too familiar — Georgia Southern's 1986 football team boarding a bus and heading for somewhere, anywhere. Southern had spent so much time away from home — nine weekends of the fifteen-game season — that the names "Greyhound" and "Trailways" belonged on the roster. At least the trip this time was a short one.

As the Eagles left their hotel in Fife, Washington, a tiny town just east of Tacoma, a group of well-wishers chanted, "One more time! One more time! One more time!" It sounded like such a simple request, yet they were asking the Eagles to do what no team had ever done — repeat as the Division I-AA national football champions.

Though the trip to the Tacoma Dome downtown was only five miles, it was of epic proportions in another way. Five years earlier, Georgia Southern's athletic department didn't even have a football program. Then, in a matter of months, the school hired Erk Russell as its head coach, borrowed a football from a nearby sporting goods store, and found the quarterback, Tracy Ham, who would propel a dream into reality.

On the road to the Tacoma Dome, looking at Mt. Ranier and its 14,410-foot, snow-capped peak over their shoulders, if any of Southern's players were dazed by the symbolic mountain they had climbed, they didn't show it.

"I can't figure these guys out," Russell had claimed weeks earlier. "They're the most loosey-goosey group I've ever been around. Nothing seems to bother them."

GSC wide receiver Tony Belser remembers the mood: "We were all relaxed. We were so confident. We didn't feel any different about the game."

"This team was as ready to play a football game as any I've ever seen," GSC assistant coach Pat Spurgeon says. "We thought we had a job to do. We were just quietly confident from about three in the afternoon on."

The game itself was set for 8:09 P.M., Pacific Standard Time, which meant for those watching the game back home in Statesboro, the kickoff would be at 11:09 P.M. Three hours, three thousand miles, and a world away.

Statesboro, the seat of Bulloch County, is bordered on all four sides by miles of farmland. The primary crops are corn and soy-

Georgia Southern's fans have had a lot to cheer about

beans, but locals will tell you that gnats grow better than anything else. The tiny two-winged insects can bite or sting, but mostly they just annoy people, especially on a hot day following a rain. Like many of Georgia Southern's football players, they're puny but persistent. Very persistent.

The crime rate in Statesboro and the surrounding small towns in South Georgia is low, but then again, there isn't that much to steal. People talk about "two Georgias," how the opportunities, the schools, the money just aren't as good in South Georgia as they are in the north closer to Atlanta.

For the most part, they're right. But Georgia Southern's success in football is helping to change that. Enrollment is increasing at the college and Statesboro is booming, but GSC's success on the gridiron has touched far more than just Statesboro.

A winning football team has given the people of South Georgia something to rally around, to point to with pride because the achievement has been theirs.

Look at the Eagles' roster from the 1985 and 1986 national championship teams. With few exceptions, the players are home-growns — from Swainsboro, Elberton, Sandersville, Waycross, Vidalia, Hepzibah, Reidsville, Wrens, and such. With the advent of Georgia Southern football, those players didn't have to go far from home to make their mark.

Most of the high schools in the area are small, so many of the players Georgia Southern used to build a national champion were overlooked by bigger schools. Unless a player had the mind-boggling statistics of a Herschel Walker, who came from nearby Wrightsville, it was hard to get noticed.

But Eagle head coach Erk Russell and his assistants mined the area close to home and turned rough bits of coal into diamonds. Somehow, GSC was able to prosper with a 215-pound defensive lineman, a five-foot-nine fullback, and a kicker who outweighed them both, proving there is more to a football player than pounds and inches. And there's no way to measure heart.

Few experts had given the Eagles any chance of repeating as national champions, and in fact the road to this second championship game had been as precarious as any August afternoon in Statesboro. Some folks had even called it a miracle, but miracles are not planned — they just happen.

2

A Rocky Beginning, A Noble Undertaking

Georgia Southern College's football program was carefully planned. It started as an idea in President Dale Lick's mind in 1978 and blossomed in 1981 with the hiring of Bucky Wagner as athletic director.

But the rest of the story just happened. No one *planned* on hiring Erk Russell, one of the most respected football coaches in America, as head coach. And no one *planned* on Tracy Ham, cast as a defensive back by most college recruiters, becoming one of the greatest quarterbacks ever to play college football. And certainly no one *planned* Georgia Southern's winning two consecutive national football championships.

Those things just happened, as miracles do.

To fully understand the scope of the miracle, one must go back to December, 1941, back to a day that lives in infamy in American history.

When the Imperial Army of Japan bombed the U.S. naval station at Pearl Harbor and the United States officially entered World War II, the call for able-bodied men was sent throughout the land. Among those that answered were the majority of the 1941 Georgia Teachers College Blue Tide football team.

In a frivolous moment, war might have seemed like a good alternative to many of them, for the team was far from successful. During the fall of 1941, the Blue Tide, under the direction of B. L. "Crook" Smith, posted a 2-8 record, defeating only Middle Georgia and South Georgia State and losing seven times by shutout. Not many of the games were close, either. Mississippi Southern downed the Blue Tide 67-0, and Oglethorpe defeated them 53-0. The other losses were to South Georgia State, Mercer, Troy State, Erskine, and Camp Croft.

Losing was nothing new to the Blue Tide. They had last experienced a winning season

Southern's first team—the 1924 Georgia Normal School Blue Tide

in 1933 when they posted a 5-4 record, and from 1924 to 1941 they had only four winning seasons.

So in 1946, when World War II ended, basketball returned to Georgia Teachers College as did baseball and a handful of other sports. But not football. The athletic department simply decided to let football die, and no one seemed to mind.

The subject of football surfaced periodically over the next fifteen years, but it never came under serious consideration. It was more a topic of conversation, a way to pass the time, than a dream worth chasing. Besides, Georgia Teachers College had become a small-college power in basketball and baseball. J. B. Scearce's basketball teams posted ten straight winning seasons from 1948 to 1957, including six twenty-win seasons. J. I. Clements' baseball teams posted eight straight winning seasons from 1952 to 1959.

The school was experiencing athletic success, so why bother with a football program? Everything was going fine without one.

On December 9, 1959, Georgia Teachers College was officially renamed Georgia Southern College to keep pace with its ever-changing curriculum. Since World War II had ended, the school's nickname had been the Professors — hardly a name to strike fear in opponents — but a new nickname was needed with the name change of the school.

By a vote of the student body, Eagles was picked, narrowly edging out Colonels.

By 1961, the topic of football had again resurfaced. Basketball coach J. B. Scearce proposed the idea to then-president Zach Henderson, who told Scearce to look into it. Scearce did by sending out fifteen questionnaires to schools of comparable size, asking if Georgia Southern started a football program, would that school play them. One said yes, one abstained and thirteen said no. That

11

Southern's first coach, E. G. Cromartie, addresses the 1924 squad

overwhelmingly negative response effectively killed the notion of football at Georgia Southern.

Basketball and baseball continued to thrive into the early 1970's, as did the new sport on campus — golf. Football remained something that was played up in Athens and Atlanta on fall Saturday afternoons.

Nate Hirsch, who became the play-by-play announcer for Georgia Southern in 1970, spent his Saturdays like most people in Statesboro.

"I would watch the big game on TV on Saturday afternoon," said Hirsch. "We would have a scoreboard show at the station in the afternoons, and that was about it for college football."

The area was not without football, though. Southeast Bulloch High School played its games on Friday afternoons, Statesboro High School played on Friday nights, and Portal High School played on Saturday nights. Enough football to satisfy most anyone.

Anyone, that is, except Dale W. Lick.

3 | Licking His Chops For A Football Team

Dr. Dale W. Lick became president of Georgia Southern College in 1978. Through the first year of his presidency, he spent much of his time traveling around the state of Georgia, meeting people and discussing the problems of Southeast Georgia and what Georgia Southern could do to help. Three questions constantly arose:

— What about university status for the college?
— What about a nursing program?
— And what about football?

Lick went to war with the Board of Regents over university status but could not win. It is still a thorn in his side and one of the few battles he lost during his seven-year tenure.

He was successful, however, in starting a nursing program to help alleviate the severe shortage of nurses in the rural areas of Georgia.

He then turned his sights on college football.

Ric Mandes, director of institutional development, traveled with Lick through much of the new president's first two years. One dark

night on a rural part of Highway 17, Lick posed a question that would change the history of Georgia Southern College.

Mandes was driving his big yellow Cadillac, Lick sitting in the passenger's seat. The two were returning from a civic club meeting in Brunswick. Lick kicked off his shoes and crossed his legs underneath him, Indian-style, and asked Ric, "What about this football thing?"

Mandes told him of J. B. Scearse's look into it back in the 1960's and explained how the question had surfaced sporadically over the years. Beyond that, no serious research had ever been done.

"Well, Ric, we need to do that," said Lick. And Georgia Southern's football program was conceived. No big fanfare. No big announcement at a banquet. Just a short question in a big Cadillac on a dark highway in the backwoods of Georgia.

Mandes fully realized that Lick was about to lead Georgia Southern College into an unknown, unexplored corner of college athletics. The drive down that highway that night was symbolic. Mandes steered and Lick watched as the headlights illuminated the mysteries that lay ahead.

13

President Dale Lick, the driving force

The first thing Lick did was establish a committee of townspeople, athletic officials and college officials to study football. Businessman Bo Hook was named as chairman, and the group was divided into six sub-committees — finance, marketing, facilities, equipment, personnel and scheduling.

Each committee researched its area and reported its findings to the other sub-committees. Lick sent out a memo to all the committee members prior to the start of their research reminding them of their purpose. It read:

"The purpose of this committee is to do research into all vital and necessary areas concerning the structure and design for intercollegiate football at Georgia Southern. There has remained for the past twenty years one dominant sports question relating to Southern: What about football? Let's answer that question now as a result of the work of this committee. The answer, regardless of 'go' or 'no go,' must be accurate and right!

"Our approach to this question will take time. We have that. Subcommittee work will be necessary and will, through this approach, provide us with specific information on which to build our complete picture. We should keep in mind the purpose of our work: to provide all of Georgia Southern — her alumni, friends, faculty, students and various other constituencies — the answer to whether football can and should be a program of intercollegiate activity at Georgia Southern."

The committees were formed in February, 1980. The finance committee consisted of chairman Hal Averitt, along with Bill Cook, Albert Parker, Lloyd Joyner, Myra Jo Oliff and Gene Crawford; marketing — Pamma Cope, chairman, with Frank Tilton, Ric Mandes, Robby Stephens and Bill Bolen; facilities — Ed Eckles, chairman, with Thurman Lanier, Joe Kennedy, Pat LaCerva and Wilson Groover; equipment — Bill Scofield, chairman, with George Cook, Earl Lavender, Charlie Wireman and Barbara Morrison; personnel — Charlie Gentry, chairman, with Pat Cobb, Mike Long, Doug Leavitt and Charles Webb; scheduling — Skip Aldred, chairman, with Hank Schomber, Gordon Alston, Nate Hirsch and Donna Henderson.

For the next nine months, the committees researched and compiled data. Surveys showed that the faculty at Georgia Southern was against the idea by a slight margin, while the community was in favor of it by an equally slight margin.

After reading the first bits of information from the committee, Lick had his doubts.

"I gave the idea about a twenty-five percent chance of succeeding at first," said Lick. "The faculty was on the fence. The town was on the fence. It could go either way and I just didn't think it would go. But I didn't say anything about my gut feeling. I waited to see what else the committee would come up with."

In November of 1980, the committee was still unsure of what to recommend. The study had been going on for ten months, and Lick felt it was time to do something. He told the committee to give him a proposal that he could work with, to put down on paper what they thought as a whole about the idea of football. A five-point proposal was made:

The Football Committee recommends that Georgia Southern College seriously consider beginning a football program in the fall of 1981 under the following conditions:

1. That the football program be financially viable; that the start-up costs can be met through independent funding, and that an annual budget be developed which will not be detrimental to other areas of the College.

2. That the development of the football program at Georgia Southern College not have a negative impact on the other athletic programs or academic programs of the College.

3. That the Georgia Southern College football program begin at the highest divisional level practical and that in the future the program move toward an even higher level of competition as finances and other circumstances permit.

4. That the College secure appropriate outside consultants to develop and implement the football program.

5. That the football program be developed consistent with all rules and regulations of the National Collegiate Athletic Association.

The proposal was given to Lick. It was now in his hands.

Bucky Wagner walked into a hot situation. He was named athletic director at Georgia Southern in January, 1981, after the football committee had made its report and before Dale Lick had decided what to do with it. He was the man in the middle, having to answer a lot of questions on a subject he was still learning about. But he handled the pressure well, just as he had done before in his career.

Wagner came to Georgia Southern from Vanderbilt, where he was Assistant Athletic Director in charge of business and tickets. He had overseen the refurbishing of Vanderbilt's football stadium and the fiscal affairs of the department. Prior to that, he had spent several years at Florida State serving in both the athletic and administrative departments of the college. He was an assistant football coach and academic advisor to all athletes for three years and then moved to the position of Director of Student Matriculation Affairs. He also served as Acting Dean of Student Services for a short period of time. A native of Ohio, he had attended Sandy Valley High School in Magnolia, excelling in football, basketball and track. He then went to Ohio University, where he first learned to handle pressure.

"I was a quarterback in high school and decided I wanted to play football at Ohio," said Wagner. "I went to a meeting and told them I was a quarterback. They told me to get in line. I was the ninth quarterback listed out of nine guys when I first got there. That's how I got stuck with the number nineteen. They gave the first guy number eleven, the second guy number twelve and so on until they got to me."

But Wagner kept working and eventually became the starting quarterback. In 1960 he led his team to the NCAA College Division national championship. Not bad for a ninth quarterback. He handled the pressure of winning a national title, and now he was handling the pressure of an embryonic football program.

* * *

Buck Wagner announces the resurrection of Georgia Southern football

Lick to Wagner: 'Here's the ball. Take it and go.'

Dale Lick read and re-read the committee's findings, looking for an answer to the question about football. The more he read, the more he liked the idea.

"The school did not have a rallying point," said Lick. "We were successful in other sports, but there is something about football that really gets people moving in the South. Georgia Southern needed football, and when I realized that, the answer was easy."

On April 9, 1981, Lick made his decision official. Georgia Southern would start an intercollegiate football program, division undetermined, and begin playing in the fall of 1981.

It was a bold decision for Lick. Georgia Southern owned no football equipment, no jerseys or uniforms of any type, had no players and no coach, but the school was going to do it anyway.

For forty years, Georgia Southern College had wandered with little athletic direction, without a rallying point. And now Dale Lick had given it one — a football team, a team that Georgia Southern could call its own. No more driving to Athens or Atlanta. No more huddling around a radio listening to Larry Munson or Al Ciraldo. Georgia Southern had its own team.

Now they needed a coach to lead them out of the athletic wilderness.

4

The Man For The Job: Erk Russell

Erk Russell was a football legend in the state of Georgia. He had spent fall Saturdays for the past seventeen years prowling the sidelines for the University of Georgia. Usually clad in black pants and a black windbreaker with the sleeves cut off, Erk represented the heart and soul of the Bulldogs. Mention Georgia football and often Vince Dooley's name was not the first one to pop up. Erk Russell's was.

His defenses were legendary. The Junkyard Dogs. The Wonder Dogs. The Under Dogs. He was, without a doubt, the most beloved sporting figure in the state — a man whose scowl could strike fear into anyone but whose heart, as the adage goes, was "gooder than gold."

His players spoke of him in reverent tones. Said one former player at Georgia, "Next to my daddy, I love Erk Russell more than any man alive."

One morning in early April, 1981, Dale Lick called Frank Inman, former offensive coordinator at Georgia and now athletic director for the school system in Brunswick, to inquire about a man who had applied for the head football job with the Eagles.

"What are you looking for in a coach?" asked Inman.

Lick told him: A winner. A man with integrity and honesty. A man who will get the people of South Georgia excited about Georgia Southern football.

"Sounds to me like you need Erk Russell," said Inman.

"That would be great," said Lick. "But we don't have a prayer of getting a coach of that caliber."

"Don't be so sure," said Inman. "Don't be so sure."

Lick had lived in the state of Georgia for only three years, and although he knew who

The community pledged its support

18

Erk Russell was, he could not fully comprehend the mystique the man carried. Lick decided to find out what he could about him.

"I attended a social gathering at Doug Leavitt's house the day after I had talked to Frank," said Lick. "I didn't hint to anyone that Erk Russell might be a candidate for the head job here because I wanted to find out what people said about him.

"A group of fellows were standing around talking about the football program and who the coach would be, and Erk's name came up. I said, 'Tell me about this guy. I don't know much about him.' And they started talking and talking and talking about what a great coach he was, what a great motivator he was and what a great person he was. So I told them maybe we ought to hire him at Georgia Southern. They all laughed and said there was just no way. I smiled and said they were probably right. The next day I got on the phone to Athens."

Lick called Georgia President Fred Davison and Athletic Director Vince Dooley to get their permission to talk to Erk. They granted it without hesitation.

In their minds, there was no way that Erk Russell would leave the University of Georgia, which had won the 1980 national championship, to start a football program at little Georgia Southern College. The thought or the possibility of that happening was foreign to them. Erk leave Georgia? Never. He had passed up far better opportunities in the past.

Davison and Dooley did one thing wrong, though. They sold Dale Lick short. When he gets his mind set on something, it usually gets done. Lick is a mover, a shaker, a man who refuses to sit still.

With permission in hand, Lick called Erk. An appointment was set. The wheels were in motion.

* * *

Erk: A great motivator, a great person

There was a lot on Erk Russell's mind as he drove on I-16 toward Statesboro. He had a meeting with Georgia Southern College President Dale Lick to discuss the possibility of starting a football program at the school.

A few months earlier, the University of Georgia had won its first national championship with a victory over Notre Dame in the Sugar Bowl. That championship was a milestone for Russell and gave him cause to think that it might be time for a new challenge. Maybe this was it.

There wasn't a lot of traffic on I-16. Not wanting to be late for the meeting, Russell pushed the gas pedal. Just as he neared the Metter exit, a state patrolman pulled him over.

The officer immediately recognized Russell. It seemed that everybody in Georgia did.

"He asked me where I was going, and when I told him I had a meeting with Dr. Lick to talk about a potential football program, he said, 'Don't keep that man waiting — but be careful.'"

Russell's meeting with Dr. Lick was at the Statesboro Holiday Inn. As the two ate lunch and discussed Lick's dream, Russell asked Lick at what level he'd like to play football. Lick said Division I.

"I thought he was crazy," Russell remembered. "I mean, I'm not sure he knew what it involved when he said that."

When word spread around Athens that Russell was considering the job at Southern, several people tried to talk him out of leaving. Dooley reminded Russell he could coach football at Georgia for as long as he liked. "Most people thought I was crazy to leave,"

Frank Inman (standing) was instrumental in getting Erk to Southern

Russell said. He talked the matter over with his wife Jean and their two sons, Jay and Rusty. All three told him to do what he wanted to do. He usually did.

"I was concerned before I met Erk," said Lick. "All the stories about him butting heads with his players and being something of an unorthodox motivator, I wasn't sure that this was the type of man that we wanted to lead our program or the type of image we wanted for Georgia Southern."

Five minutes over lunch at the Holiday Inn changed that attitude.

"I listened to the man for five minutes," said Lick, "and I realized that he was a man of great integrity and honesty. I knew right then that we needed Erk Russell. I just had to convince Erk that he needed us."

Before he was a coach, Erk Russell was an athlete. Growing up just outside of Birmingham, Alabama, Russell lived for sports. He'd race home from school, change clothes, then play whatever was in season — basketball, football, or baseball. He was also pretty good at marbles and horseshoes. His first coach was A. J. Killebrew, a math teacher at Ensley High who coached several sports at the Ensley YMCA. After graduating from Ensley High, Russell went on to become the last four-sport letterman at Auburn, playing football, basketball, baseball and tennis.

"Honest to goodness," Russell says, "I wasn't very good at any of the sports. I came along at a time when there wasn't much competition."

Once, as a basketball player for the War Eagles, Russell hit two long set shots in the final minutes to beat Southern Illinois, 50-48. "I felt like I owed the team that much since my man had scored forty-six of Southern Illinois' points," Russell quips.

As a football player, he played end and led the War Eagles in receptions in 1948 and '49, and he still holds the school record for the highest yard average per catch in a single game with three catches for 118 yards, or 39.3 yards per catch, in a 1949 game against Georgia.

Years later, at age thirty-eight, he was a good enough athlete to reach the quarter-finals of the Athens City Tennis Tournament.

During his college days, Russell began to lose his hair. Eventually he began shaving his head. After graduation, he coached football and basketball at Grady High School in Atlanta, where he was twice named the Class AAA football Coach of the Year. In 1958, he returned to Auburn as a graduate assistant and coached the freshman football team and the varsity baseball team.

One day, as he led the Auburn freshman football team up the hill to meet the varsity for the first time in fall practice, the son of an Auburn football secretary pointed to Russell — clad in white shorts and a T-shirt — and shouted, "Look, Mama, there goes Mr. Clean."

The nickname stuck, but Russell didn't. In 1963 he left Auburn to become the defensive coordinator at Vanderbilt. One year later, when fellow Auburn alumnus Vince Dooley was named the head coach at Georgia, Russell called Dooley up.

"Vince, how about a job?" Russell said.

Though the 'Dogs had an occasional down year, Russell always seemed to be able to get the most out of his athletes. To inspire them before games, he would butt heads with his linemen. They would be wearing helmets — all Russell had for protection was his freckled scalp.

Ric Mandes (right) was Lick's right-hand man in dealings with Russell

Even though he was nearly three times as old as his players, Russell was still intimidating. A cutoff T-shirt revealing strong arms was a Russell trademark. When tempers flared in a Georgia Tech-Georgia contest, Russell was one of the first to jump in to stop the brawl.

His players identified with Russell and played their hearts out for him.

In 1967, the Bulldogs were the Southeastern Conference leader in total defense and scoring defense. In 1968, the Bulldogs led the SEC again in total defense and the nation in scoring defense. In 1969, Georgia was sixth in the nation in scoring defense and led the SEC in pass defense. From 1967-71, Georgia's scoring defense was second in the nation. In 1976, the 'Dogs led the SEC in scoring defense. In 1978, Georgia trailed only national champion Alabama in scoring defense — by a single point. In 1979, the 'Dogs led the nation in takeovers. In Georgia's national championship year of 1980, they led the nation in turnover margin.

During those successful years, Russell was often wooed as a head coach, but he never found an offer attractive enough for him. At least, none attractive enough to leave a good situation at Georgia.

But the Georgia Southern opportunity was different. It came on the heels of Georgia's 1980 national championship and seemed to be the right time for Russell.

Erk had been to Statesboro only a handful of times. Prior to his interview with Dr. Lick, he'd never been to the Georgia Southern campus. Once he'd been asked to speak to a local booster club. Another time he came to see Statesboro High play. One other time, he came to recruit a running back for Georgia.

But it wasn't Statesboro that attracted Russell. It was a chance to do something new.

"I felt that I needed a change of responsibilities and challenges," Russell remembers. "I felt that, really for the first time, I may have been looking out the same window too long. I needed to do some different things. When I looked at this situation at Georgia Southern, I could see new challenges and responsibilities, and I felt like I needed those things.

"This was starting from zero, from the ground. No tradition, no helmets, no football. You couldn't find a situation where you could say, any more than right here, this is mine to do or die with."

The events of the next three weeks would later be called by Dooley "the best recruiting job I've seen in twenty-five years." Erk was treated like royalty in Statesboro. Everywhere he went, people watched him in awe. Erk Russell in Statesboro? Erk Russell at Georgia Southern? Some found it almost too good to be true.

Davison and Dooley began to squirm. Every newspaper in the state speculated on Erk's decision. "Erk to Leave for Georgia

A crowd of several hundred came to hear Russell accept the challenge

23

Southern," one headline would shout, while another would read the exact opposite.

Steve Brunner got the real story.

Brunner had been a student at Georgia Southern and was working as a sportswriter for the *Statesboro Herald* while Erk was the constant topic of conversation in Statesboro. On Thursday, May 21, Brunner received an anonymous call saying that Erk was on his way to Dale Lick's office. Brunner grabbed his notepad and headed for campus.

"It was late in the afternoon or early evening," said Brunner. "The campus was empty when I wandered into the administration building, and the door to Lick's office was locked. But I decided to wait around in the hallway and see if anything happened.

"There was a table out in the hallway next to Lick's office, so I sat on it waiting to see if Erk or Lick showed up. It turned out that they were in Lick's office and, for some reason, from where I was sitting I could hear every word that was said between the two of them. I don't know if the walls were thin or the sound was carrying well because the building was empty or what, but I heard Lick ask Erk when he wanted to announce it, and Erk said, 'Let's do it Monday.'"

President Dale Lick couldn't hide a smile of satisfaction

B. L. 'Crook' Smith coached the '41 Eagles; forty years later he finally got a successor

Brunner waited around until Erk emerged from the office. Knowing that Erk had taken the job, he wanted something official. But Erk wouldn't give it to him. He left town without a word.

Brunner hurried back to the office and wrote his story that Erk would be hired and that the announcement would come Monday. Satisfied with himself, he packed his bags for a weekend vacation. He would be back on Monday for the announcement.

When the *Herald*'s story hit the stands on Friday morning, Statesboro began buzzing like a swarm of August gnats. The proverbial cat was out of the bag. Erk was coming to Georgia Southern.

With Brunner's story in print, Lick and Erk changed plans and scheduled a press conference for Saturday at 10 A.M. In announcing the press conference, Erk's name was not mentioned, but Statesboro knew what was about to happen.

Roger Inman, equipment manager for the athletic department, spent all of Friday night painting a backdrop — the Eagle emblem — for the stage. Jim Radcliffe and some friends

25

A hand goes up, a program is reborn

had T-shirts printed with an Eagle holding a football and the words "Erk's Eagles" emblazoned underneath.

Meanwhile, a light rain fell on Statesboro. In the parking lot of the Southside Beverage Company, Ric Mandes sat in his yellow Cadillac waiting for the rendevous. Erk, who had sneaked back into town, pulled up next to Mandes. The drivers faced each other in the darkness.

"Let's go in my car," Mandes told Erk.

Russell parked his car, bought a six pack of his favorite beverage (Budweiser) at the store and climbed in. Mandes started driving aimlessly. Russell took a swig and looked at Mandes. "You know, Ric, I must be the craziest man alive. I just spoke in Wrightsville tonight, and in the parking lot at the high school, I said good-bye to Herschel Walker. *I* said good-bye to Herschel Walker. I've got to be crazy."

By 9:30 A.M. Saturday, the lower stands of one side of Hanner Fieldhouse were filled with Georgia Southern fans. In the athletic offices behind those stands, Erk sat with Dale Lick, Bucky Wagner and Mandes, going over the itinerary for the press conference. Suddenly Mandes' face went blank as he realized he didn't have a football to use as a prop. The school didn't own one. Mandes called Frank Hook at Sports Buff, a nearby sporting goods store, and asked him to bring one over in a hurry.

At 10 A.M., the quartet walked onto the floor of Hanner Fieldhouse, and the several hundred people who had gathered inside erupted into a crescendo of clapping, cheering and whistling. They had read the stories about Erk's coming, they had heard the rumors. But it wasn't official until he walked into the gym.

For five minutes, they cheered. And when they had finally quieted, Bucky Wagner stepped to the podium.

"I would like to introduce the first football coach at Georgia Southern in forty years — Erskine 'Erk' Russell." Wagner handed the brand-new football to Erk. Russell thrust it into the air with his right hand, and the people cheered loud and long again.

"If I had known there was going to be a crowd here," said Russell, "I would have gotten a haircut."

Georgia Southern football was reborn. And somewhere in the state of Georgia, Steve Brunner, the man who had broken the story that Erk was coming, was taking a break and eagerly awaiting a press conference on Monday.

5

And They Called It Football

Three months before Georgia Southern's first football practice in forty years, the official inventory of the program consisted of one football and one head coach. That was it. No helmets, shoulder pads, jerseys, pants, shoes, socks, jocks, thigh pads, hip pads, knee braces, chin straps, assistant coaches or players.

So athletic director Bucky Wagner and equipment manager Roger Inman took one of the athletic department vans and headed off on a four-state scavenger hunt. They drove to the University of Mississippi, where they were given some cast-off jerseys, helmets and shoes. They then drove to Vanderbilt and got some more hand-me-down gear. On to Georgia Tech, Florida State and Georgia. Anything related to football that they wanted to give away, Wagner and Inman gladly accepted. Meanwhile, Erk busied himself with lining up a coaching staff — two full-time assistants and four graduate assistants.

On September 28, the first day of practice, 134 players wandered out of Hanner Fieldhouse and walked down to the practice fields.

Erk called them "134 of the most enthusiastic non-athletes I've ever seen." There were no scholarships to be given out, no one had been recruited. All 134 of them had walked into Erk's office during the previous couple of weeks saying they wanted to play football. One was a student from Germany who had never played the game but thought he could kick. One was a 5-8, 150-pounder who had been an offensive lineman in high school, and another was a 6-0, 200-pounder wearing horned-rimmed black glasses and walking with a noticeable limp.

But they all wanted to play college football. They all wanted to play for Georgia Southern. They all wanted to play for Erk Russell.

Erk later said, "That was the most fun I've ever had coaching. Those guys didn't have any talent. All they had was desire. They wanted to be there. I'll take a group of guys with a bad case of the wants any day."

On that first day of practice, Erk wore a T-shirt that read, "Eagles — GATA." For print, GATA means "Get After Them Aggressively." In fact, it means "Get After Their Ass."

Mike Healey was one of the first assistant coaches hired by Russell. He had been a successful high school coach in Jacksonville, Florida, before Erk persuaded him to come to Georgia Southern.

"That was a rough bunch of football players," recalled Healey. "And our equipment was terrible. The shoulder pads were kind of thin. Some of the players brought their own shoes. We had a blocking sled that we had gotten from a high school. It was broken, but some guys from Plant Operations had come over and welded it back together. About twice a week, the welding would break and we'd call 'em and they'd come over and re-weld it.

"We even had a couple of guys practicing with us that weren't even in school. We found out about it and had to ask them to leave. It was rag-tag beginnings."

On October 31, 1981 — Halloween, appropriately enough — the Eagles played their first scrimmage at the Shamrock Bowl in Dublin with the White team winning, 28-17.

The curtain goes up . . .

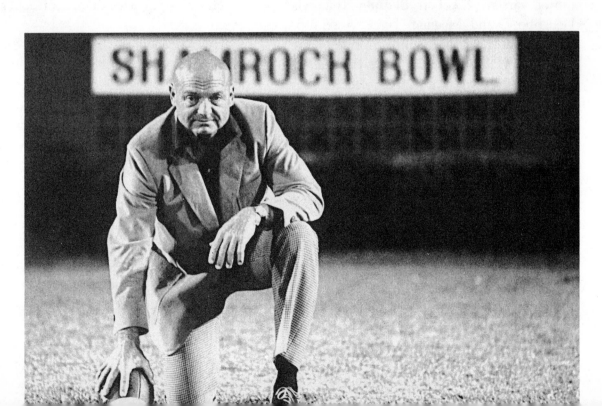

Wayne Bulluck led the game in rushing, gaining eighty yards on twelve carries for the Blue. Rob Allen paced the White by completing six of ten passes for 126 yards and one touchdown. For the record, the first play of the new era was a Rob Toole kickoff to William Carwell, who returned it from the ten to the thirty-yard line. Allen scored the first touchdown, a one-yard run, and Bobby Matheny kicked the first extra point. A crowd of 2,006 paid to see it. Georgia Southern football had officially begun.

"That game looked like an all-star game of sorts," recalled equipment manager Inman. "We had been given helmets from Ole Miss, Vanderbilt, Georgia Tech and Georgia, so everybody was wearing different color helmets. Some of the jerseys were light blue and some were dark blue and all of them had holes in them, but we had fun."

The offensive lines of both teams combined averaged 203 pounds per man; the biggest was Fred Feinstein, who tipped the scales at 225 pounds. Only one player, Daryl Fineran, was taller than six feet.

That team later played the Florida State junior varsity, the Fort Benning (Georgia) Doughboys, and Magnum Force, a semi-pro team from the Jacksonville, Florida, police department. The Florida State JV beat the Eagles, 30-20. Steve Rogers led Georgia Southern with fifty-seven yards rushing. The Eagles evened their record at 1-1 with a 33-26 win over Fort Benning. Rob Allen passed for 162 yards and three touchdowns to lead Southern. In the season finale, the Eagles whipped Magnum Force, 49-27. William Carwell rushed for eighty-two yards and two touchdowns to pace Georgia Southern.

* * *

A handful of scholarships was available for the next season, the first eleven-game season for Georgia Southern. The season opener was slated to be Central Florida in Jacksonville's Gator Bowl. The Eagles eventually won the game, 16-9, but that they even got to play was due in part to some fast talking by Roger Inman.

Georgia Southern didn't have a truck to carry all the equipment to Jacksonville, so Inman contacted a friend who lent him a horse trailer. Inman and his three assistants loaded up the trailer and set off for Jacksonville on I-95.

Inman was driving down the interstate when he noticed a state patrol car behind him, lights flashing. He pulled over and the patrolman approached the truck. A horse trailer is considered an agricultural vehicle, and all such vehicles are required to stop at weigh stations on the highway. Inman had driven right past one, and the patrolman was a bit upset.

"What are you carrying?" inquired the officer.

"Football equipment," replied Inman. The patrolman stood with a look of doubt on his face.

Inman opened the back of the trailer for the patrolman to inspect. Among the shoulder pads and helmets stacked in the trailer sat the three managers, each holding a handful of cards with several dollar bills scattered on the floor between them. Patrolmen frown on gambling as much as they do running weigh stations.

Inman talked fast and managed to get out of the situation with just a warning. On the return trip that night after the game, the horse trailer broke down and a wrecker had to tow it in. On the next road trip, Inman rented a regular truck.

Southern's first scrimmage, with players outfitted in mismatched helmets and hand-me-down pads

Erk was an instant hit with fans of all ages

The Eagles posted a 7-3-1 record that year, defeating Central Florida, Baptist 42-0; Fort Benning, 56-6; Newberry, 36-14; Mars Hill, 17-3; Valdosta State, 45-29; and scoring a revenge win over the Florida State JV, 31-20. They lost to Catawba, 10-7; Wofford, 28-7; and Gardner-Webb, 44-6; they tied Valdosta State, 27-27.

A few of those first-year players raised some eyebrows around Statesboro, particularly a kid named Tracy Ham at quarterback. He ran the offense with reckless abandon, cutting upfield at a moment's notice and heaving passes while on the run. But he fumbled the ball a lot. Bad hands, most people said. Might have to move him somewhere other than quarterback.

The 1983 season was Georgia Southern's first full schedule against all four-year schools. No more Florida State JV or Fort Benning, and Magnum Force was almost a forgotten name.

Again, Georgia Southern opened the year against Central Florida, but this time they lost, 33-29, an omen of things to come. The Eagles wound up the year 6-5, losing four games by five points or less. The wins came over Presbyterian, Gardner-Webb, Catawba, Wofford, Mars Hill and Savannah State. The losses were to Central Florida, Troy State, East Tennessee, Newberry and Valdosta State.

Ham had become the starting quarterback in 1983, but he still lacked consistency. The fans didn't seem to mind, though. The program was only two years old, and everyone realized there was room for growth.

Tracy Ham knew he had some growing to do. Not physically, but mentally. He was the starting quarterback, and he needed to improve before the 1984 season began. No one could have imagined the scope of that improvement.

6

A Hairy Introduction To I-AA

Russell's first office was a makeshift mobile home

Erk Russell knew something about his 1984 Georgia Southern team, but he didn't want to tell anybody. Instead, he let his hair speak for him.

Ricky Mehaffey covered Georgia Southern for the *Savannah News-Press*. Three days before the season opener, he wrote, "Georgia Southern has as much chance of having a winning season as Erk Russell does of growing hair." Consider Mehaffey's point. Southern football had played as an unclassified club sport in 1982 and 1983 against mostly NAIA schools. This season, they were embarking on their first year in the NCAA's Division I-AA, the second toughest division in all of college football. Included on the schedule were traditional I-AA powers Florida A&M, Middle Tennessee State, UT-Chattanooga and East

In addition to being head coach, Erk was also Southern's primary fund raiser

Carolina, fresh off an 8-3 season in I-A and ranked twentieth by *Sports Illustrated*. The odds didn't look good.

But Erk couldn't waste the opportunity to use Mehaffey's story as a motivational tool for his players. The story appeared in the Wednesday morning paper. That afternoon, Erk showed up at practice wearing his usual cutoff baseball pants and a white T-shirt with a hole cut out of the middle, exposing a healthy crop of chest hair.

He walked over to Mehaffey, who was covering practice that day, and said, "Ricky, I can grow hair with the best of them. It's just poorly proportioned." And with that statement, Erk's Eagles embarked on their first season of I-AA football.

Allen E. Paulson Stadium was supposed to be ready for the September 1 season opener against Florida A&M. However, rainfall had been far above normal during the summer, causing construction to fall behind by three weeks, so the game was moved to Savannah's Memorial Stadium.

The Rattlers of Florida A&M were a team of mystery to Georgia Southern fans. They had never seen the Rattlers play, but they did know that they had won the I-AA national title in 1977 and that, traditionally, they were a very strong team.

"If we can just play them close," said one fan, "that'll be good."

Ticket sales were not going as well as expected, so officials at the Georgia Southern

35

athletic department decided to pay the Florida A&M band $7,000 to come to the game. The Marching 100, Florida A&M's band, is without a doubt the nation's most entertaining college band. They play impeccably, and the formations and dance routines they perform require as much athletic skill as it takes to play football.

Ticket sales soared when it was announced that the Marching 100 would be in Savannah. Nearly thirteen thousand fans showed up to watch. The fans who came to see a great football game saw a great halftime show, and the fans who came to see a great halftime saw a great football game.

Tracy Ham connected with Monty Sharpe on a fifty-four-yard touchdown pass, and Tim Foley booted the extra point to give Georgia Southern a 7-0 lead late in the second quarter. As it turned out, those were the only points the Eagles would need that day. But for good measure, Ham scored on a three-yard run late in the third quarter, and the Eagles went on to win, 14-0.

Georgia Southern demolished Presbyterian the following week, 41-6, as Ham ran for one touchdown and passed for two more. The Eagles then traveled to Orlando, Florida, to face Central Florida. That game was a hint of things to come.

Melvin Bell scored on an eighteen-yard run in the first quarter, and Gerald Harris scored from three yards out in the second quarter as the Eagles posted a 14-7 halftime lead. From that point on, both defenses were out to lunch.

Ham hit Sharpe on a forty-four-yard strike to extend the lead to 21-7, but the Knights answered with a touchdown to cut it to 21-14. Ham hit Sharpe again, this time from thirty-one yards away to build the lead to 28-14, only to see Central Florida score four minutes later on a ten-yard strike. Each team

had scored on each possession of the third quarter. That fifteen minutes of football set the standard for Georgia Southern for the next three years. Run it, gun it and simply outscore the opponent. Southern had found its identity.

Dexter Sanford and Gerald Harris scored in the fourth quarter, and the Eagles went on to win the game, 42-28.

The Eagles were 3-0 and about to play the biggest game of the young program's history. East Carolina was the opposition, off to a slow start at 0-3 but still a I-A team.

Despite being a twenty-four point underdog, Georgia Southern came within inches of upsetting East Carolina. A furious Eagle rally was thwarted on the game's last play when a Tracy Ham pass was tipped four times in the end zone before being intercepted by Kevin Walker. The interception secured a 34-27 East Carolina win.

The interception was one of very few Ham mistakes. He completed twenty-six of fifty-two passes for a school record 403 yards and two touchdowns. He directed the offense to another school record 645 total yards, the most in NCAA history by a losing team.

The Pirates stunned the Eagles early, scoring twenty-one unanswered points in the first quarter. But Georgia Southern responded in the second quarter with a four-yard touchdown pass from Ham to Robert Baker and a twenty-five-yard Tim Foley field goal.

East Carolina again took a twenty-one point lead in the third quarter, 31-10, but again the Eagles fought back. Ham connected on a thirty-two-yard screen pass to Gerald Harris for one score, and Harris later scored on a two-yard run. Coupled with a thirty-nine-yard field goal by Foley, the Eagles cut the lead to seven before falling short on the last play.

A master motivator and creator of slogans, Erk describes his 1982 team

Baker ended the day with a school record nine catches and Sharpe had seven. The East Carolina fans were enthralled with Ham. As he did his post-game interviews outside the Georgia Southern locker room, several Pirate fans stopped by to shake his hand. One fan said to Ham, "That was the greatest display of courage and guts I've ever seen. Son, you're a hell of a ballplayer. You'll do well."

In the press box upstairs, the chief statistician was burning up the batteries in his calculator adding Ham's yardage. "I've been doing stats here for a long time," he said, "and that is the second-best quarterback I've ever seen on this field."

"Who was the best?" asked a bystander.

"Terry Bradshaw," the man said.

Allen E. Paulson Stadium was finally ready to be unveiled. There would be no more home games at Womack Field at Statesboro High School. The Eagles had their own field, their own stadium, their own place to play, and they wanted to inaugurate it in proper fashion.

"When we walked out of that locker room and saw that stadium filled with people," said wide receiver Delano Little, "we felt like the greatest team in the world. The sun was shining, it was a beautiful day. There was no way we were going to lose."

The Eagles routed Liberty Baptist, 48-11, before 12,097 fans, and the inaugural game went off without a hitch. Everything at the stadium ran to perfection. The concession

stands did a brisk business, the bathrooms worked and the Eagles won. Allen Paulson couldn't have diagrammed it better himself.

The Eagles, in what was becoming a typical game, outscored Bethune-Cookman, 43-33, in the Gator Bowl the following week, lifting their record to 5-1. People outside of Statesboro started to take notice. On Monday after that game, the NCAA ranked Georgia Southern as the seventeenth-best team in Division I-AA. Only six games into its first season in the division, the Eagles were considered a national power. The fans went wild, as did the players. All over a seventeenth ranking. No one knew what lay ahead.

Bolstered by the ranking, the Eagles upset UT-Chattanooga, 24-17, at home, then whipped Newberry on homecoming, 41-16, and Valdosta State, 38-8, the following week. And with each win the Eagles climbed in the polls. They moved to fifteenth after the UT-Chattanooga win, to thirteenth after the Newberry victory, and with the slaughter of Valdosta State, they moved into the top ten for the first time at No. 7.

Erk didn't like all the attention his team was suddenly getting.

"We can't sneak up on people anymore," he said. "The higher we're ranked, the more the other team will want to beat us. I don't like polls for that reason. When I was at Georgia, we used to say, 'You know what dogs do to poles.' Now that I'm an Eagle, I guess I'll have to say that me and the other Eagles have a better angle on the polls on which to do our stuff."

Russell stalks the sidelines while Eagles storm the field

The euphoria that had gripped the team and its fans came to a screeching halt in the next two weeks, though. Tracy Ham threw six interceptions as the Eagles lost to East Tennessee State, 20-17, and then in a game marred by heavy rain, they closed out the season at Murfreesboro by losing to Middle Tennessee State, 42-7.

When the final top-twenty poll came out, the Eagles were nowhere to be found. An 8-3 record wasn't good enough to crack it, and other I-AA teams forgot the Eagles. They were a flash in the pan, a shooting star that illuminated the I-AA sky for just a moment, then withered and died. Or so those teams thought.

But the 1985 season was on the horizon, and the sun would shine bright on the Georgia Southern Eagles and their quarterback, Tracy Ham.

The inimitable Tracy Ham

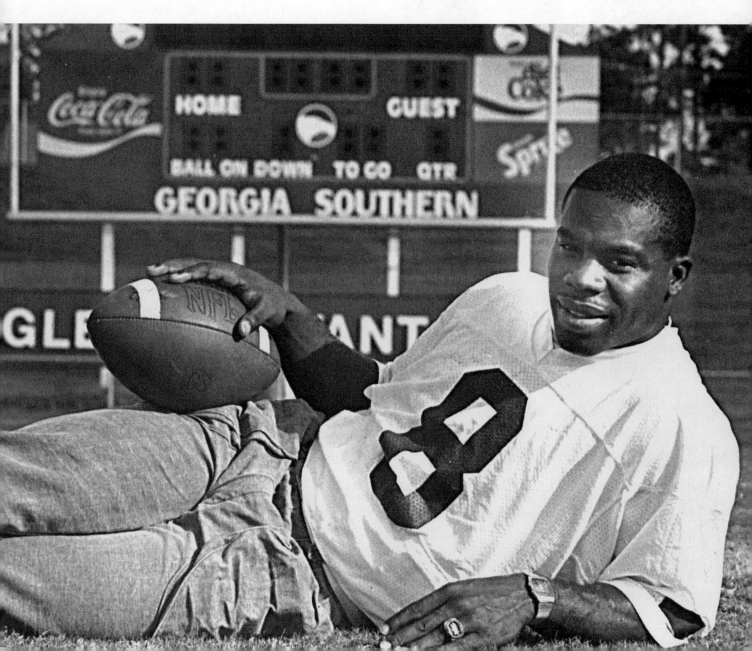

7 | Tracy Ham—The Color In Southern's Rainbow

Disappointment showed on Tracy Ham's face. It was noticeable because it was uncommon to his usual happy-go-lucky appearance. He sat slumped in a chair in Erk Russell's office, and even though he wouldn't admit it, he seemed almost uncomfortable.

It was February 1987, and Tracy had just returned from a National Football League scouting combine — a meat market packed with would-be professional football players being watched closely by a gaggle of scouts representing every NFL team. He had spent three days at this one in Indianapolis running with a football, catching a football and dodging imaginary tacklers.

But the one thing Tracy didn't do in Indianapolis was *throw* a football.

"I got there and they had me listed as an OH — offensive halfback," said Ham. "I did what they wanted me to do, but it felt weird getting down in a stance. I haven't done that since I was a freshman in high school. I ran good. I didn't hurt myself as far as the scouts are concerned. But it sure felt different."

Although Tracy Ham one day may be a great running back in the NFL or even a wide receiver or defensive back or kick returner, it's not what he was meant to be.

He was disappointed that day because he knew he wasn't a running back. And anyone who ever saw him play would say the same thing.

There was little interest in Tracy Ham when he was a senior at Santa Fe High School near his hometown of High Springs, Florida. A few schools wrote letters to him and a few others talked to him about playing college football — as a defensive back. The word quarterback was never mentioned, and why should it have been? He wasn't even considered the best quarterback in the county his senior season. He was voted second-team All-Alachua County behind a player whose name has long since been forgotten.

On one occasion, an assistant coach from Valdosta State College sat in a coach's office at Santa Fe, a national letter-of-intent on the table and a pen in Tracy's hand. He talked about all the great things that Tracy would be able to accomplish in a Blazer uniform, and just before Tracy signed on the dotted line, the assistant coach said the words that changed the history of Georgia Southern football.

"Tracy," he said, "we're looking forward to

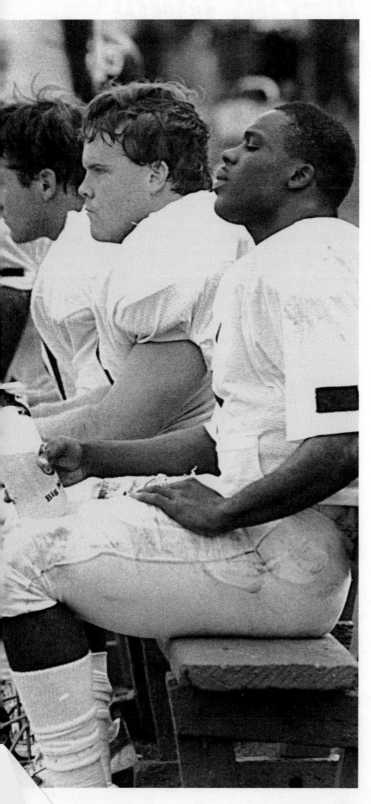

Ham watches from sidelines along with
Charles Cochran, Ronald Warnock

having you play for us because we consider you to be a top athlete, and we want to put our best eleven athletes on defense."

Tracy placed the pen on the desk and said thanks, but no thanks.

Even though no school had talked to him about playing quarterback, he knew that was the position he was meant to play. Mike Healey thought so, too.

Healey was one of the first assistant coaches hired by Erk Russell. He had been head coach at Archbishop Kennedy High School in Jacksonville, and when the time came for Georgia Southern to find a quarterback, Healey told Russell about this kid from High Springs that he had coached against a year earlier.

"I remember watching him on film," recalled Healey. "During the entire game that night we played them, I kept waiting for him to break one or throw the big pass."

Russell told Healey to give him a call. Healey then traveled to Santa Fe High School and talked Tracy into visiting Georgia Southern. There was no fanfare, no headline about Ham's visiting Statesboro. After all, he was just an unknown second-team All-County quarterback no one wanted.

Tracy told Russell that he wanted to play quarterback. Russell said fine.

It was eight games into the 1982 season before Ham became the starting quarterback. Before then, the Eagles used him at running back, and he also returned kicks and punts. That changed against Valdosta State. Ham returned the opening kick in that game and then stayed on the field and played quarterback.

"That was the last time I returned a kick," said Ham. "I guess the coaches thought it looked a little strange with me returning the kick and then just staying on the field."

Ham began the 1983 season as the starter and never relinquished the job. He guided the Eagles to an average 6-5 record but showed flashes of brilliance that caught Russell's eye.

"It didn't take us long to realize we had something special," said Russell. "The thing that really stood out about him was his ability to turn a nothing play, a dead play, into something. He was a good option quarterback; a good short passer, quick, good at reading defenses, very smart on the field. But he had something more.

"When we realized that, we were willing to go all-out and feature his ability. We knew if we put him into the position to direct things, to show what we had, that he'd just get better and better. I don't have to tell you how he responded."

The "Hambone" offense was born, and I-AA football would never be the same.

Most people think Russell nicknamed the offense the Hambone, since he's been known to think up a clever monicker or two. But not this one. It came from Steve Brunner, sportswriter for the *Savannah Morning News*.

On November 16, 1983, Brunner coined the phrase that would become a household word among the Georgia Southern faithful: "Some teams run the wishbone and others use the wingbone, but Georgia Southern relies on the Tracy Ham-bone," wrote Brunner. "It's a simple offense, really. All a team needs is a quarterback who can break an option play seventy-five yards, throw cruise missiles and psychoanalyze opposing defenses. Ham . . . does all of the above."

The Hambone was designed by former offensive coordinator Ben Griffith and refined by his replacement Paul Johnson. It was a wide-open, fun-to-watch offense from the Georgia Southern sideline. From the other side of the field it was a nightmare.

Only once during Ham's senior season was Georgia Southern held to less than twenty-eight points. The Hambone averaged 41.3 points per game and more than five hundred yards in total offense.

But don't think the Hambone was just Ham. There were other ingredients — Gerald Harris, Ricky Harris and a great offensive line, to name a few. But it was Ham who triggered everything in the touchdown-happy offense.

Ham spent five years at Georgia Southern dancing, dodging and baffling opposing defenses and winning virtually every award a I-AA player can receive. He was named the *Atlanta Journal-Constitution* College Player of the Year three times and its Amateur Athlete of the Year twice. Following his senior season, he was a consensus All-American choice, making all three I-AA teams — Kodak, Associated Press and *Football News*. He was *Football News* Offensive Player of the Year. He was tabbed Player of the Year in 1986 by the Atlanta Touchdown Club, Macon Touchdown Club, the 100 Percent Wrong Club of Atlanta, the Georgia Sports Hall of Fame and the Georgia Sportswriters' Association. He was a finalist for the prestigious Davey O'Brien Award (the only I-AA quarterback among the top-ten finalists) and he led the East team in rushing in the 1987 East-West Shrine Classic in San Francisco.

During his regular-season career, he became the first player in college football history to rush for more than three thousand yards and pass for more than five thousand yards and became the first player in I-AA history and only the fourth overall to rush for a thousand yards and pass for a thousand yards in the same season. He holds more than fifty Georgia Southern records and five

NCAA records. He led the Eagles to two consecutive I-AA national titles, accounting for more than ten thousand yards in total offense in his career. And in his final thirty games as Georgia Southern's quarterback, he led the team to a 26-4 record.

And no one wanted him as quarterback except for Georgia Southern.

However, there is more to those numbers than just footnotes in a football record book. Tracy Ham didn't simply pile up statistics against weaker teams. He always saved his best for the big ones, the games where everything was riding on it.

The two I-AA championship games are perfect examples. Tracy Ham's biggest games at Georgia Southern were not against Wofford or Mars Hill or Catawba, but against Furman and Arkansas State and East Carolina.

In the 1985 championship game against Furman, Tracy compiled a career high 509 yards in total offense, passing for four touchdowns and running for one.

In the 1986 title contest against Arkansas State, he gained 486 yards — 180 rushing and 306 passing — and threw for two touchdowns and ran for three more.

In two games against Division I-A East Carolina, Ham gained 742 yards, including an NCAA-record 199 yards rushing in the 1986 game.

In eight playoff games in two years at Georgia Southern, the Eagles never lost. The last eighteen games that Ham quarterbacked the ·Eagles against I-AA opponents, Georgia Southern never lost. The list goes on and on.

So much has been written about the ability and unpredictability of Ham that it would take the better part of a day to sift through the newspaper clippings. Here are some of the better quotes about Tracy Ham:

— "If you could open him up and take out his chemistry, you might find a cure for cancer." (Boots Donnelly, head coach, Middle Tennessee State)

— "They (Arkansas State in the 1986 I-AA championship game) thought they were going to play another football game. Instead they entered the Twilight Zone, where Ham takes you into the unknown and scares the daylights out of you." (Pete Wickham, staff reporter, *Memphis Commercial Appeal*)

— "You can't tackle smoke." (Larry Lacewell, head coach, Arkansas State)

— "I know we'll send Ham a graduation present. Every I-AA school probably will." (Larry Lacewell, again following Georgia Southern's 48-21 win over Arkansas State in the 1986 title game)

— "Tracy Ham is to Georgia Southern what colors are to a rainbow." (Mark Johnson, staff reporter, *St. Petersburg (FL) Times*)

The quotes go on and on. All with their own unique flavor but all saying the same thing — Tracy Ham was the most devastating quarterback that college football has ever known.

"I'd be lying if I said I ever believed any of this could have happened," said Ham. "When I came here, I just wanted to make the team, hopefully get some playing time. I felt if I got in the lineup and contributed something to the team, that would be all I could ask for."

He asked for little. He got a lot. And it took him a long way from the sandlots of High Springs, Florida.

Growing up wasn't easy for Tracy. He was the youngest of six children — two sisters and three brothers. His mother died when he was just three years old, and his grandmother, Idella Dunbar, raised the family.

Tracy spent his idle hours playing sandlot football with his brothers and friends. He was always the smallest and, consequently, had to try harder just to keep up with the bigger boys. He used to tell them that he would play football at the University of Florida some day. The Florida campus was only twenty minutes away.

That wish came true when Ham quarterbacked Georgia Southern in the 1986 season opener against the Gators. It wasn't a dream come true, however, as the Eagles lost, 38-14.

To Georgia Southern College, Tracy Ham is more than just a football player, more than just a *great* football player. He is the foundation of a fast-growing football powerhouse.

"How can you possibly evaluate what Tracy has meant to this school?" said Athletic Director Bucky Wagner. "How can you put a yardstick on his contributions? All you can do is look around, see the success of the institution and the athletic program and realize that football has been a big part of it. And that Tracy Ham has been a big part of the football team.

"To say he wasn't extremely important to us, to say that he wasn't the key to all our

'You can't tackle smoke,' an opposing coach said of Tracy Ham; (opposite) Fans answer the question 'Where's the beef?'

success . . . well, that just wouldn't be telling it like it is. I just look in the scorebook and see that in four years, Tracy Ham didn't play in six quarters, and we didn't score in any of them."

In addition to all of the honors, awards and recognition that Tracy has received, he was given the ultimate compliment in 1987. On February 4, Georgia Southern College retired his jersey. No one will ever wear that blue-and-white No. 8 again. And no one should. The sight of anyone else in it would destroy memories that Georgia Southern fans hold too dear.

Remember No. 8 scrambling frantically against Furman on that last touchdown march, avoiding tacklers, and finding Tony Belser to keep the drive alive, giving everything he had for the sake of winning.

Remember No. 8, circling around right end against Nicholls State in 1986, sprinting fifty-five yards for the touchdown, always coming up with the big play when Georgia

Southern had to have one.

Remember No. 8 twisting and turning and stretching his muscled frame for just one more yard against Nevada-Reno, trying to pull off just one more miracle.

Remember No. 8 heaving a fifty-yard pass to a streaking Monty Sharpe against Northern Iowa in 1985.

And remember No. 8 rifling a desperation pass to Frankie Johnson against Furman.

And remember how you felt each time. Watching him move would take your breath away, and just when you had given up hope, he would find a way, he would create a miracle, he would gamble and win, and you screamed and yelled and cheered with the loudest of them. Not because Georgia Southern had done something good, but because No. 8 had made the impossible possible.

Remember it and relish it. Relive each moment, and cherish them all.

Remember Tracy Ham, for the likes of him will never pass this way again.

Last Shot At Being A Champ

Jessie Jenkins had always wanted to be a champion. During his junior year, Warner-Robins High School was beaten in the Georgia Class AAAA playoffs by Tift County, which went on to the state championship. His senior year, the Demons were ranked No. 1 in Georgia and even rated as one of the top teams in the nation, but they were upset in the playoffs by Lowndes County, which went on to win the state title. Ironically, Warner-Robins won the state title the following year — after Jenkins was gone.

The loss to Lowndes his senior year was more than disappointing. In the game, Jenkins suffered cartilage damage and stretched ligaments in his left knee. With the injury went his chances of a scholarship to a Division I school. Florida had shown some interest, and Clemson had talked of using the 6-1, 200-pounder from Bonaire, Georgia, as a linebacker.

Despite a successful operation on his knee, Jenkins' doctor, Fred Allman of Atlanta, advised him to quit football. Jenkins had no intentions of doing any such thing. With the aid of a state-of-the-art contraption called the Lenox Hill brace, named after an Atlanta hospital, Jenkins was able to walk on at Georgia Southern on September 28, 1981.

That was Georgia Southern's first day of football practice since 1941. Head coach Erk Russell was attempting to restart a program that had been dormant since Pearl Harbor. All 134 players on the first day of practice were walk-ons.

"There were guys there who didn't know how to put knee pads and thigh pads on," Jenkins said. "Coach Russell had so many assistant coaches out there. A lot of those guys were ex-players from Georgia, and I really looked up to them."

Larry West, a high-school teammate of Jenkins, was a bit overwhelmed at the number of players. There were twenty-six offensive guards. By the last day of practice that summer, there would be two, including West.

"I was only 195 pounds and it seemed that everybody was bigger," West said. "They had players from every place; some of them had been in the Army and were a lot older. Some of them didn't even know how to run."

The equipment, to be generous, was not first-rate. Many of the helmets, thinly disguised hand-me-downs from Mississippi and Georgia Tech, were the older suspension models instead of the modern air cushion helmets. "You could really get your bell rung easily," West said.

Jenkins was a cut above some of the other players there. Russell told the collective troops, "Look to your left. Look to your right. And in front of and in back of you. Chances are those people won't be here next year."

By the start of the next season, there were only twenty players remaining from the original 134. Five years later, at the beginning of the 1985 season, Jenkins was the only original Eagle left.

It was his senior year, so if he wanted to be a champion, this would have to be the season.

Jessie Jenkins, last of the original Eagles, led the '85 team in tackles

Tracy Ham (flanked on the left by Danny Durham and on the right by Ricky Harris) became a media favorite

The summer before the 1985 campaign had been a rough one for Georgia Southern. When Georgia head football coach and athletic director Vince Dooley talked of running for the U.S. Senate, the first name that came to mind to replace him was Erk Russell. Never one to hedge, Russell said he'd be crazy not to consider becoming the next head coach at Georgia, if the job was offered. After an agonizing wait while Dooley made up his mind, Statesboro breathed a collective sigh of relief when, on July 25, Dooley announced he'd decided against running.

With the first day of fall practice came the next crisis. Melvin Bell, the Eagles' all-time leading rusher, had gained 1,969 yards in three years. But he'd injured his neck during the summer and reinjured it during a vertical leap test. He'd decided to leave the team, to quit football.

With Bell gone, the starting tailback job went to Ricky Harris, who soon would have people asking, "Melvin who?"

As the weeks wore down prior to the Eagles' first game against Florida A&M, Russell reminded his players the season was near by telling them how many days were left until the opener — every day he told them, like counting off the shopping days left until Christmas. Finally, it was time for the last workout, a light run-through on Friday. At the end of practice, everybody ran wind sprints. For a little extra incentive, the players from Florida voluntarily ran an extra set of sprints.

Bordering the St. Johns River in Jacksonville, Florida, the Gator Bowl brings back memories of many wild Georgia-Florida games. GSC's first game of the 1985 season was against Florida A&M in the Gator Bowl, making it something of a mini Georgia-Florida bash. The Eagles' roster that day included five players from Jacksonville, so it was also nearly a home contest for Southern.

First-game jitters were evident from the opening series. Southern had the ball on its first possession for exactly four seconds as Ham fumbled his first snap. A&M quickly gave the ball back as sophomore linebacker Tyrone Hull intercepted Mike Kelly's pass. But once again, a bad pitch by Ham allowed FAMU to take possession.

After Danny Durham's second sack of the day, the Eagles got the ball back, only to fumble it again. Ham first bobbled it, and after Ricky Harris recovered, he fumbled.

At that point, Russell was actually toying with the idea of sitting down his star quarterback, who was having one of his worst days as an Eagle, and bringing in freshman Ernest Thompson.

But Ham finally got in sync. He capped an eighty-yard drive with a thirty-seven-yard touchdown to Monty Sharpe. After FAMU tied with a touchdown of its own on an eighteen-yard alley-oop pass from Kelly to Robert Gentile, the Eagles took a 10-7 lead with a fifty-yard field goal by Tim Foley with two seconds left in the first half.

Early in the third quarter, Ricky Harris took it eight yards on a pitch and scored,

giving GSC a 17-7 lead. With Harris pounding away for his game-high 117 yards, the Eagles were able to set up two more scores, a thirty-three-yard field goal by Foley and a five-yard run by Gerald Harris, giving GSC a twenty-point lead with 13:10 remaining.

It was almost not enough. GSC was going with a new cornerback, junior-college transfer Chris Aiken, and Kelly was picking on him. Earlier in the game, Gentile had out-leaped Aiken for FAMU's only first-half touchdown. With the Eagles worrying about the pass, the Rattlers crossed GSC up when Kelly ran twenty-nine yards for a touchdown on a broken play. Another touchdown run by

Melvin Bell was Southern's 'Mr. Versatility'

51

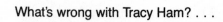

on his heels, that meant he was preparing to pass block, and Richardson would nod to Rossignol to drop back to defend the pass. An offensive tackle up on his toes usually was enough of a sign for Richardson to signal Rossignol to help against the run. Richardson didn't need to clue Rossignol this time. Down by a touchdown and deep in his own territory, there was little doubt Kelly would try to air it out.

In the closing moments, Richardson sacked Kelly twice. The second sack wrapped up the win for GSC with only four seconds remaining.

After the game, it was a mob scene as relatives surrounded the players trying to get on the buses. Ham vowed to do better. He would need to, considering who the Eagles would play next.

Antonio Barber, this one a three-yarder with 4:20 left, brought FAMU to within a touchdown of winning.

But in stepped John Richardson, who was playing in front of his hometown crowd. He'd spent a great deal of his summer not far from the Gator Bowl, working on the docks of the St. Johns River. It was the same job he'd chosen over going away to college, even though he had offers from Middle Tennessee State and Tennessee State. He didn't want to play football at the time, but after two years of working and going to junior college, his mind was changed by Erk Russell and Mike Healey.

Known more for his ability to stop the run, Richardson turned pass rusher with the Rattlers going for broke. He and rover Hugo Rossignol had a signal going. When Richardson noticed an offensive tackle rocking back

Middle Tennessee State represented a mountain for the Eagles. On the last game of the 1984 season, Southern went to Murfreesboro, Tennessee, needing a win over MTSU to earn a playoff bid in their first year of I-AA competition. The host Blue Raiders drubbed Southern 42-7 in a blinding rainstorm, scoring twenty-two points in the fourth quarter. After the game, Russell gave his players a rare dressing down.

But this year things would be different. Though coached by Russell to remain modest to the press, in private Eagle players talked of things as heretical as an undefeated season. At the very least, they knew they were an improved team over the past season, and this time things would be different when they faced the Blue Raiders.

Russell actually angered a few of his troops when he told the media he was "afraid" for his players and that this was too big a game too soon. In a private meeting with the team, however, he set them straight.

"That's just for the newspapers' benefit," Russell said. "I don't believe a word of that and neither should you."

Maybe he should have. Once again, Middle Tennessee came right at the Eagles on offense and were unstoppable.

Early in the first quarter, a fumble by Ham gave MTSU the ball at Southern's forty-two and the Blue Raiders scored. After a field goal by Tim Foley, another GSC first-quarter blunder put Southern in the hole, 14-3. Rob Whitton's punt was blocked and rolled out at the ten. Three plays later, Gerald Anderson scored from the two. When quarterback Marvin Collier scored on a fifty-four-yard run

three plays into the second half, GSC was in trouble against the Raiders' ball-control offense.

GSC didn't score a touchdown until the fourth quarter. The Eagles' top rusher was Ricky Harris with only fifty-one yards. Ham had thirty net yards and, despite throwing for eighty-one yards, was intercepted twice in eighteen attempts. In something of a moral victory, GSC was able to move the ball. Despite the lopsided score, 35-10, the Eagles were outgained by only three yards of total offense.

Again, people were asking what was wrong with Ham. Collier, who was from Crisp County High School in Cordele, Georgia, spoke his mind after the game.

"They say he [Ham] is the best quarterback in Georgia. Well, I think I showed them something today."

Actually, Collier's statement was rather strange since Ham was actually from Florida and played in Georgia and Collier was playing for an out-of-state school. Regardless, it was pretty brash stuff from a redshirt freshman, and it would come back to haunt him before the season was over.

The route from Statesboro to Troy, Alabama, home of Troy State, the defending Division II national champion, zigzags across rural areas of middle Georgia and Alabama. Once you get to Troy, cotton is still king, as it once was over the entire South. It is prevalent enough that it grows wild on the side of the road in Troy.

It took the Eagles more than the usual amount of time to get to Troy as one of the team buses, carrying most of the defensive team, was delayed en route by two flat tires.

. . . Not a thing in the world

53

Russell was more nervous than usual during the days before the game. It was the type of situation he hated. Though the Trojans were the reigning Division II champions, they were still the underdogs. His teams always played better, looser, as the team nobody expected much from. Russell didn't like the shoe on the other foot.

Unfazed by their coach's nervousness, GSC's players contented themselves with lounging around the hotel pool. The daytime heat in Troy was stifling, but the game would be played at night.

The squads were nearly mirror images of each other. Like Southern, Troy State relied on the familiar wishbone, which was not that much different from GSC's Hambone-I. Both were option attacks.

Troy State was known for its powerful ball control offense, and that was definitely a concern for GSC's defenders and defensive coordinator Mike Healey. There was something else about the Trojans that concerned GSC — their no-huddle offense.

But that turned out to be in Southern's favor.

"Their quarterback would call the plays at the line of scrimmage," Healey said. "After the first quarter, Jessie Jenkins was able to determine where the ball was going, because he'd figured out their offense. It was like in World War II, when the United States broke the Japanese code on the wireless."

"The quarterback would go to the line of scrimmage and call a play, like 'Blue 36,'" Jenkins said. "Since they ran the wishbone, everything started with the fullback. The way I'd always been taught, all even numbers were to the right and all odd numbers were to the left. You could also tell if they were going to the strong or the weak side. I couldn't believe they didn't change, because they had to know I had them figured out."

While Jenkins was busy making nineteen tackles (fourteen of them solo tackles) with his inside knowledge, Southern's own offense wasn't that hard to figure out. Troy State was taking away the fullback dive and the tailback pitch, two of the Eagles' three options. That left the third option — Ham by himself.

After his less-than-stellar performances in the Eagles' first two games, Ham was taken aside by Russell, who talked to his junior quarterback about a lot of things but mostly about leadership and how he needed Ham to produce it. Ham had always been a leader of sorts. Along with Ricky Harris and Monty Sharpe, it seemed as if Ham had invented the word "relax." Russell didn't want to curb Ham's enthusiasm, but he wanted his young quarterback to know if Southern was going anywhere, Ham was going to have to do the driving.

Beginning with the Troy State game, Ham put things in gear and didn't stop until they had to carry him off the field a few months later.

Once again, Southern fell behind early, but a thirty-seven-yard field goal by Troy State's Ted Clem five minutes into the game was answered seven minutes later by a twenty-five-yarder by Tim Foley.

Ham put the Eagles up to stay with a drive that started at the end of the first quarter and rolled through part of the second. Ham ran left for two. He completed a pass for sixteen yards to Delano Little. Ham jitterbugged right for thirteen yards. He handed off to Steve McCray for four. After being stopped for no gain at the Trojans' seven, Ham ran again, and this time he snuck it in from the right side for a touchdown.

Both teams continued to move the ball but could find the end zone only once each in the second half. Southern's big break came mid-

Hugo Rossignol (28) makes another crucial interception for Southern

way through the third quarter when Charles Carper picked up Troy State quarterback Mike Turk's fumble at the ten. A few plays later, Ham connected on a rare screen pass to Gerald Harris for the touchdown.

But Troy State caught the Eagles playing cautious and drove eighty yards in nine plays with Tommy Dugosh scoring from the Eagles' one to cut Southern's lead to 17-10 with 3:10 left.

Troy State had already shown a lot of character by handcuffing GSC. Other than Ham, who would wind up with all but sixty-two of GSC's 314 yards of total offense, the Eagles had been stymied. But Southern's defense had been stingy. Now the Eagles would need to hold Troy State off one more time. Those three minutes would seem like weeks.

Hugo Rossignol, a 5-10, 210-pound senior, was a product of Bishop Kenny High School in Jacksonville. His head coach then was Healey, one of the first coaches selected by Russell in 1981. Rossignol had gone to East Carolina but transferred to Georgia Southern in 1982 to be closer to his father, who had suffered a heart attack earlier that year. Rossignol had always been close to his father, who ran a mini-blinds business in Jacksonville. After graduation, that commitment to family carried over into his work as he became a surveillance officer for the Chatham County Juvenile Court.

Rossignol wasn't the only former Division I player on the team. Offensive tackle Vance Pike and linebacker Beau Brown (another Bishop Kenny grad) had been at Auburn while offensive tackle Jeff Evans was a transfer from Louisiana State.

"Misfits — that's what we looked at ourselves as," Rossignol said. "The other teams would always make comments about us, said we couldn't play somewhere else. We loved it when they did that. I loved making guys eat

their words. It was like a mission."

Rossignol's mission at the moment was to prevent Troy State from scoring. After driving to Southern's forty-one with approximately two minutes left, Turk attempted to pitch out, but Rossignol got a hand on the ball and tipped it out of bounds. But the Trojans kept coming. After a pass from Turk to Dugosh for ten yards, Turk ran for ten more yards two plays later to the GSC twenty-four. Time was running out, but Troy State was getting close. A touchdown and a two-point conversion could win it for the Trojans. After Ted Horstead ran for five yards and one yard, Troy State lost five yards on an illegal procedure penalty. On third and nine, Turk didn't see anybody open and ran for two yards.

Faced with a fourth-and-seven, it was do or die for Turk and the Trojans at the GSC twenty-one. Rossignol looked in Turk's eyes and was surprised when the quarterback kept looking straight at Dugosh. There was little question who the intended receiver was, but Rossignol beat him to the spot. Interception! Rossignol returned it twenty-three yards before Troy State jumped on him first and then his own teammates tackled him for joy.

But the Eagles couldn't just run out the clock. They had to have a first down. After Gerald Harris ran for six yards on first down, he went up the middle again, only to be stopped for no gain. On third down, Ham stepped back as if to pass, fooling nobody. It didn't matter; he coasted past the line of scrimmage and hurried for eighteen more yards and the game-saving first down. He fell on the ball twice after that and Southern had a winning record again.

Assistant coach Mike Healey, original equipment at GSU

Tennessee-Chattanooga would be a different type of test. The Moccasins were natural rivals for Georgia Southern for a variety of reasons. UTC was the defending champion of the Southern Conference, an organization the Eagles desperately wanted to join. As a I-AA independent, GSC had to scramble every year to fill its schedule. In the prestigious Southern Conference, GSC would have had a certain number of set games every year and would have benefitted from the intensity of conference games, which bring out more fans.

There was another reason for a natural rivalry. Tennessee-Chattanooga had always considered Georgia its own happy hunting ground for recruiting. Many of the borderline players who could have gone to Georgia Tech or the University of Georgia wound up at UTC when they found out they were merely bench fodder. Two of the Mocs' running backs, Keith Montgomery and Alan Evans, were transfers, Montgomery from Georgia and Evans from Auburn.

But in recent years, Georgia Southern had begun to make inroads on territory that was formerly UTC's, which didn't sit well with Mocs' head coach Buddy Nix. UTC, which had advanced to the first round of the I-AA playoffs in 1984, also didn't appreciate a 19-14 loss to Southern that year.

As usual, a tight defensive struggle was expected. The Mocs' didn't have much firepower on offense, so they had to play defense well to win.

Southern's own defensive strategy was simple but scary: Put the emphasis on stopping the run, which will force the Mocs to pass and maybe make a mistake. The frightening part was that pass defense was a GSC weakness. While all of the offensive starters were scholarship athletes, nine of the eleven defensive players were originally walk-ons.

The Eagles often got by on defense with fewer "natural" athletes by using players with heart. That generally worked against the run. Put nine players with plenty of guts on the defensive line, and they'll stop a ball carrier. But to defend the pass, speed is very important: quick rushers are needed to rattle the quarterback and even speedier defensive backs are needed to cover the receivers. The Eagles normally had problems with their rush, and the defensive backs were also a little on the green side.

But in this game, the pieces fell into place for the Eagles' defense. On the first play from scrimmage, Moc running back David Williams fumbled at the twenty and cornerback Chris Aiken recovered at the Chattanooga five-yard line. A few plays later, Gerald Harris rolled in from the one to put the Eagles up 7-0 with Tim Foley's point-after. A face mask penalty proved costly to GSC as a two-yard pass from quarterback Couch to Williams on third and thirteen was turned into a first down at the Eagles' twenty-four. One play later, Couch threw a touchdown pass to Alan Barner to tie the score.

From there, the defenses woke up. With linebackers Greg Moore and Spanky Thomas chasing him, Ham was sacked for a four-yard loss at his own thirty-seven, and Foley was forced to nail a fifty-four-yard field goal to put the Eagles up 10-7 with 1:02 left in the quarter.

Neither team would score in the second period as each quarterback was intercepted once. Couch put his team up 14-10 early in the third quarter on a thirty-six-yard touchdown pass to Barner. The Eagles looked like they would respond with a touchdown of their own, but after Ham passed the team to the Chattanooga nine-yard line, the Mocs' defense stiffened and Southern had to settle for a twenty-yard field goal by Foley to cut UTC's lead to 14-13.

Again, it was defense that set up the winning score for Southern. On the first play of the fourth quarter, Couch made a bad pitch and John Richardson recovered at the Chattanooga thirty-two. Ham passed to Ricky Harris for eleven yards for one first down, and two plays later Monty Sharpe beat defensive back David McCrary by a step and Ham threw a strike for a twenty-yard touchdown pass. A two-point conversion pass by Ham fell incomplete, leaving the Mocs 12:59 to respond.

Again the defenses took charge. Southern stopped UTC at its own thirty-one and Southern couldn't get a first down. After Couch was intercepted by Brad Bowen, Ham was intercepted by Moore one play later. Running out of time, UTC went for it on fourth down and five yards with 3:16 left and the ball on GSC's fourteen, but Couch couldn't get the ball to Barner.

All Southern had to do was get a couple of first downs to run out the clock. UTC helped with a facemask call with 1:33 left to give Southern a first down at its own twenty-eight. Two plays later, Ham scrambled for forty-nine yards, and then all he had to do was fall on the ball twice to end the game.

Ham once again makes something special out of nothing

9 | *Making The Playoffs ...The Hard Way*

Georgia Southern and Tennessee Tech were like two trains passing in opposite directions. At one time, the Golden Eagles were a power. In a nine-year stretch from 1952-61, Tech was the champion or co-champion of the OVC every year. But the glory days were gone at Tennessee Tech. The Golden Eagles were 0-11 in 1984 when head coach Gary Darnell brought in twenty-eight new players. They weren't helping much, as the Golden Eagles were 0-3 going into their game with GSC.

Like Troy State, Tech ran the wishbone. Seeing how Southern had beaten Troy State's hurry-up wishbone attack, Darnell joked, "We're going to use slow huddles. We'll just take a lot of time getting up to the line."

Darnell probably wished he'd stayed home by the time the whole thing was over. Southern won 34-0 with the GSC defense holding the Golden Eagles to one yard passing and 154 yards rushing. With GSC so effective at stopping Tech, the day became a coming out party for tailbacks Frankie Johnson and Steve McCray.

Johnson, a five-foot-nine, 175-pound freshman tailback, was a walk-on from Screven County High School in Sylvania. In high school, he had been a point guard on the basketball team. Though not much of a scorer, he specialized on defense. Frank knew what being a role player was all about. Before the season was over, he would play a very big role for the Eagles.

When school was out, nobody had bothered to sign Johnson. He talked about working someplace to help the family, but his father, Issac, a construction worker, wouldn't hear of it. He wanted his son to go to college and he wanted him to play football, even if it meant that he and his wife, who worked in the laundry room of a nursing home in Sylvania, would have to pay for their son's chance to play. Frank, the eldest of three boys, was small and not very fast, but he had something special that made him difficult to tackle.

So it was decided that Johnson would walk on at Georgia Southwestern, a Division II college in Americus that GSC assistant coach John Pate had helped to start. But Johnson's football coach at Screven County, Sandy Hershey, had also seen that something special in Johnson, and he wanted something better for his player. Nearly every day, Hershey would pester GSC offensive coordinator Paul

Johnson telling him about the undersized tailback. Finally Johnson was invited to walk on at Southern.

That summer, Frank Johnson worked at a supermarket in Sylvania and then at a gas company in Jenkins County to help earn money for school. When fall practice began in August, his room and board were taken care of by the football team — but only until school started.

Against Tech, starting tailback Ricky Harris was a little banged up, so Russell called for Johnson. His first carry ever as an Eagle was for thirteen yards. The second time he touched the ball, he ran for a fifty-seven-yard touchdown, the longest touchdown run from scrimmage of the season. Johnson ran through a big hole provided by blocks from Herman Barron and Monty Sharpe and found himself alone with the Tech safety. Instead of trying to outrun him, Johnson cut back across the grain, giving his blockers a chance to catch up, and then Johnson's path to the end zone was clear.

With six more carries, Johnson became the game's leading rusher with 122 yards. McCray, a walk-on from Jacksonville who had already been granted a scholarship, scored the Eagles' next two touchdowns on runs of twenty-six yards and one-yard. A one-yard run by Ham and two field goals by Tim Foley completed the scoring.

Georgia Southern's hopes of back-to-back shutouts were ended quickly against Bethune-Cookman. BCC quarterback Bernard Hawk eventually threw forty-seven times, completing twenty-one attempts for 251 yards, a touchdown and three interceptions.

Southern didn't have to resort to such drastic measures. With Ricky Harris having his best day of the season, rushing for 154 yards and a pair of touchdowns, GSC kept adding to its lead. At one point, Southern

appeared in trouble when the Wildcats tied the game with 9:35 remaining in the second quarter.

But then Tim Foley got into the act. For the third game in a row, he had two field goals without a miss. With Southern's offense

dying twice late in the first half, he booted a forty-three-yarder and a fifty-yarder to put the Eagles on top for good at 20-14. His second field goal, coming with just six seconds until halftime, visibly demoralized BCC.

Now Hawk had no choice but to throw, and Southern quickly took advantage with linebacker Charles Carper intercepting a pass and running it back twenty-nine yards for a score just three minutes into the second half. The final was 46-24.

Frank Johnson (48) is congratulated by his teammates

With the win over Bethune-Cookman, Erk Russell found his team ranked No. 8, but it wasn't a good feeling. Russell always said that rankings could only hurt, not help, a team. The only ranking that mattered was the one after the season.

Southern had been ranked as high as seventh in 1984. Then came the 20-17 loss at East Tennessee State and the 42-7 defeat at Middle Tennessee State. With those losses, the Eagles fell out of the top-twenty rankings and their playoff chances went out the win-

During the '85 season at Southern, bald was 'in'

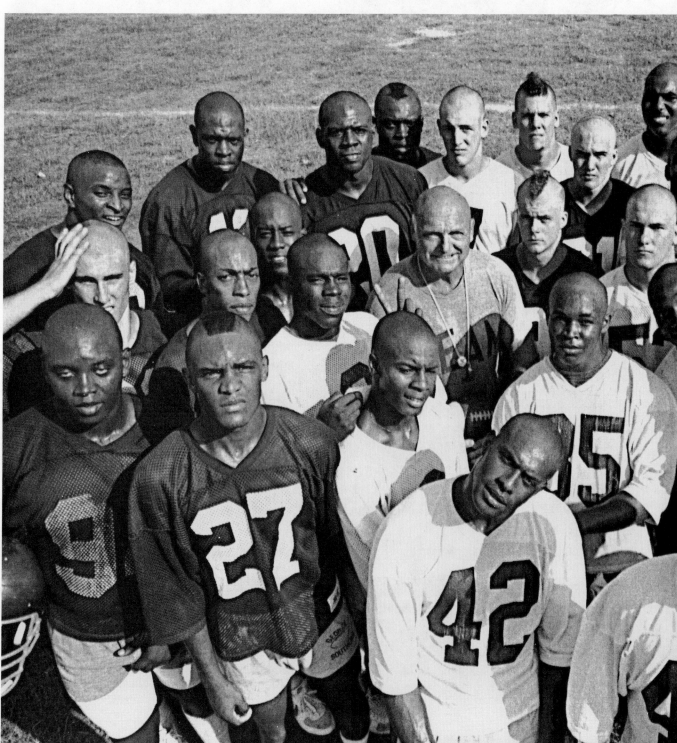

dow. It could happen again if Southern took Newberry lightly.

Though an NAIA school with just 625 students, Newberry already had one upset under its belt, a 24-21 win over perennial Southern Conference power Furman.

The game would be homecoming at Georgia Southern, and though the crowd was fashionably late, it would be the largest home

crowd in school history with 12,831 showing up, beating the previous record of 12,743 set in Savannah's Memorial Stadium.

Some of those who sauntered in late missed the only tense moment of the game — the coin toss. Southern took a 21-0 lead with 1:02 still remaining in the first quarter.

The first time Ham touched the ball, he rolled down the right sideline, waited for a few key blocks, then cut across the field one way and then another for a forty-five-yard touchdown.

After Hugo Rossignol came up with an interception at the Indians' seventeen, Ricky Harris ran for thirteen yards and Gerald Harris plowed through three times, scoring the last time from the one. A bad punt following Newberry's next possession and a twelve-yard run by Ricky Harris put the ball at the Indians' twenty-nine. Ham took over from there, running up the middle and then putting a move on cornerback Sylvester Coleman for the score.

With the aid of six Eagle mistakes in the second half (four interceptions and two fumbles), Newberry was able to look respectable in a 38-17 finish.

Southern was 6-1 when it readied itself for its longest road trip of the season to play James Madison in Harrisonburg, Virginia. The route to JMU wanders over mountains and usually pleasant scenery. But the weather was bad, with unseasonably chilly temperatures and a steady downpour. It had also been a bad year for JMU, 3-5. The team won its first two games, then dropped five straight. The week before the game with Southern, the Dukes got back on track by whipping Davidson, 28-0. There was no way for James Madison to make the I-AA playoffs, but the Dukes could play the spoiler role.

The weather stayed the same on game day. Georgia Southern assistant athletic director Hank Schomber, who drove a van of school officials and sportswriters for the game, remarked that he didn't have a good feeling about the game. As they had been a year earlier when they lost to East Tennessee State, the Eagles were seventh-ranked and were playing on artificial turf. To downplay the cold weather, Russell came out in shirt sleeves.

James Madison head coach Joe Puryzcki thought he had his team ready for Tracy Ham. He'd devised a defense he called "the Ham Jam" to limit GSC's quarterback. The defense turned out to be unnecessary.

James Madison came out fired up, stopping the Eagles on their first drive. After Southern did the same, JMU kicker Joe Henry's twenty-nine-yard field goal was wide left. The Dukes' defense, led by All-American Charles Haley, now a starter with the San Francisco 49ers, continued to give Southern problems. On third down and five, Haley blocked Ham's pass. On fourth down, he broke through the line to block Pat Parker's punt. It rolled out of bounds at Southern's seven-yard line. James Madison quarterback Greg Lancaster, who had sparked his team a week earlier in his first collegiate start, wasted little time, hitting senior receiver Rick Rice for a seven-yard touchdown pass.

Ham moved quickly to quiet the soggy crowd of five thousand, running for ten yards on second down. Near the end of the run, as he turned out of bounds, he twisted his left ankle. He was able to run twice after that before the pain began to get to him and he had to be carried off the field.

When Ham went down, so did the Eagles, who collapsed like a house of cards. In his place went freshman Ernest Thompson from Louisville. Compared to the 5-11, 185-pound

Erk's theory on practice: 'The harder I work, the luckier I get.'

64

Ham, Thompson, at six-foot-two, 205-pounds, looked like "something you'd grease up and put in front of a health spa," Russell had said.

But Thompson didn't have the players' confidence yet and it showed. The Eagles' drive stalled and Southern had to settle for a fifty-one-yard field goal from Tim Foley. Another field goal by Foley in the fourth quarter would be all the points Southern would muster as James Madison upset the Eagles, 21-6. GSC's defense shut out JMU in the second half, but that was a moot point.

Afterwards, Russell was disappointed in his team's effort and let them know it. Now the Eagles knew they had to win their final three regular season games to make it to the play-offs. And how would they do it without Ham? Thompson had completed only five passes in twenty attempts. The initial prognosis on Ham's ankle sprain was that he would be out for as long as three weeks.

A day later, the Eagles got better news. Ham might be ready to play the following weekend against Central Florida. But by Monday, there was more bad news. With the loss, GSC fell from seventh to No. 16 in the rankings. With only twelve bids available, the Eagles had their work cut out for them.

As the Central Florida game neared, Ham's ankle was still tender, though he was able to practice. Russell thought it best to keep his star quarterback out unless he was needed.

Playing without Ham in the first half, the Eagles again could not score a touchdown. To make matters worse, it was an off day for Southern's pass defense as UCF's Tony Lanham thrice found receiver Ted Wilson for long touchdown passes. Wilson had 4.3 speed, and on his first touchdown catch of thirteen yards, no one was near him. On his

second, for fifty-one yards, he blew by safety Brad Bowen. His third TD catch of the half was for sixteen yards and came even with Chris Aiken trying his best to interfere. Down 18-6 late in the second quarter, Russell could take no more.

When Ham went in, the Paulson Stadium crowd of 7,759 rose with their hopes. While Ham was obviously not at full speed, the lift his appearance gave his teammates was obvious. On the first GSC series of the second half, the Eagles rolled, with Gerald Harris soon scoring on a two-yard run. Four minutes later, Harris bounded over again from the four-yard line and Ham tossed to Herman Barron for a two-point conversion. GSC led 21-18.

Central Florida needed a quick score to stop Southern's momentum. Again, Lanham drove the Knights down the field. When UCF went for it on fourth down and six at the GSC twenty, the Eagles put the blitz on and Jenkins sacked Lanham, knocking him out of bounds.

Immediately after that, Ham found Tony Belser for a twenty-three-yard pass, somehow scrambled for another first down, this one of thirty-one yards, and then rolled out right for an eight-yard score. Another touchdown by Harris late in the fourth quarter made the final 35-18. What Ham had done couldn't be overlooked. Not only had he led Southern to twenty-two unanswered points in the third quarter, but for the first time the benefit of his presence could be measured.

"What was the difference in having Tracy in there?" Russell said. "The difference was six to eighteen and thirty-five to eighteen."

UCF head coach Gene McDowell, a little shell-shocked, said, "He's the best quarterback we've played against. It's too bad they don't play the option in the pros."

The East Tennessee State game was not a friendly rivalry. The Eagles had lost twice to the Buccaneers, and the two teams and their athletic departments weren't on great terms with each other.

Some of Southern's players were fifth-year seniors, since the NCAA did not count GSC's years of club football in 1982 and 1983 against the players' eligibility. ETSU athletic director Buddy Sasser was an outspoken critic of Southern for what he said was their unfair advantage. He may have been right, of course, but GSC officials knew they were playing within the rules of the NCAA.

Ricky Harris led the Eagles in rushing in 1985

When Eagle assistant coach Pat Spurgeon scouted ETSU's game with Marshall the week before Southern would play the Bucs, Sasser gave Spurgeon an earful of anger, calling the Eagles "outlaws."

When word got back to GSC's players of Sasser's outburst, it was like throwing gas on the fire. Southern felt it had gotten a raw deal the year before when ETSU beat Southern 20-17 in Johnson City, Tennessee. Some of GSC's players could also remember how embarrassing their 24-7 loss in 1983 to ETSU had been. That was GSC's first game against a I-AA opponent. The Bucs came out in war paint and easily intimidated Southern.

There were at least two players on the opposing teams that got along, however. GSC junior safety Brad Bowen's brother Ken was a senior linebacker for ETSU. Coming out of high school, Brad had thought about playing for East Tennessee State, but Ken had discouraged him because, at the time, the Bucs had an unsettled coaching situation. The 1985 game between the two teams, to be played in Statesboro, would be a family gathering as game day would also be a birthday for Ed Bowen, father of Brad and Ken.

If the game was a family get-together for the Bowens, it was a picnic for the Eagles. Southern romped 46-7 with Monty Sharpe catching five passes for ninety yards and five touchdowns. About the only intrigue was how much GSC's fans and ETSU's players would go at each other. A shouting match between Southern's students and the Bucs escalated into an ice-throwing contest before security officials were able to break up the melee.

* * *

The pressure was on for GSC. The Eagles' mission was simple: Beat South Carolina State in their final regular season game and the playoffs would beckon. Lose and there was always the next year.

But the options were as much on the table for South Carolina State as they were for Southern. The Bulldogs needed a win to guarantee a .500 season. A loss would probably cost head coach Bill Davis his job, for it would mean his second straight below .500 season.

The Eagles' practice sessions the week before the game kept running out of daylight with the early fall sunset. After his players began bumping into each other in the dark, Russell shortened one practice. It was suggested to him that the Eagles' practice field could make do with headlights since Southern had no outdoor football facilities with lights.

"If we make the playoffs, you'll find those type of things will take care of themselves," Russell said. "Heck, if we make the playoffs, we may still be playing while everyone else is out of school on vacation."

At least one person, Gerald Harris' mother, Cecile Harris, had faith. She told her son she wouldn't make the trip to Orangeburg, South Carolina, for the game because she was saving her trip for the Eagles' first playoff game.

Like a good son, Harris didn't betray his mother's confidence. He ran for 156 yards with touchdown runs of thirty-five, fifty-six and one yards to lead the Eagles to a 43-30 win over the Bulldogs.

But the victory wasn't as easy as it looked, for South Carolina State's offense, led by quarterback Charles Glaze, gave the Eagles all they could handle. Glaze scored from three yards out and threw for touchdown passes of seventy-nine yards and twenty yards.

Going into the final quarter, Southern led only 28-23 when it got a break.

Ham had led a drive to the S.C. State twenty-nine, but Gerald Harris committed a rare fumble. The play was called back, however, because the Bulldogs had too many men on the field. Given another chance, Tracy Ham tossed a twenty-three-yard touchdown pass to Delano Little, who made an acrobatic catch even with defender Eric Smith hanging onto his face mask.

South Carolina State came back with a score eleven plays later on a five-yard run by Gerald Foggie. A two-point conversion try failed twice. The first time the Bulldogs' fake kick became a pass that was batted down, but GSC was called for interference. The second two-point try, a run by tailback James Cunningham, was stopped at the line.

Ham quickly put Southern ahead for good. After the Bulldogs' score, Ham's first play from scrimmage was a sixty-seven-yard pass to Herman Barron, who was chased down from behind by Sam Felder. Two plays later, Ham rolled out left, pump-faked a pass and ran right to leave both teams in his wake for an eight-yard touchdown. A two-point conversion pass to Tony Belser put Southern comfortably ahead, 43-30.

The next day the Eagles found out for sure they were in the playoffs. But despite their win on Saturday, their ranking slipped from a three-way tie for No. 8 to ninth. The teams Southern had been tied with were Murray State and Grambling State. Murray State lost 27-25 to drop in the rankings, but Grambling beat Southern University to stay in eighth. GSC and Grambling had identical records. Their one common opponent, South Carolina State, had beaten Grambling 13-10 earlier in the season.

It didn't seem fair, but the Eagles were too happy just being in the playoffs.

68

10 | *Flying High With An Eye On Success*

It was an unusual ritual. To an outsider, it might have seemed as strange as the running of the bulls at Pamplona, Spain.

Before every Georgia Southern football game of the 1985 season, members of the defensive line and a few veterans, such as offensive linemen Vance Pike and Jeff Evans, would walk out of the locker room to stretch—regardless of the weather. Actually, stretching wasn't all they did, for they'd line up in a circle and butt helmets on cue like Rams fighting over territory.

On this particular day, however, the head butting was a little more intense. Finally, the Eagles were in the playoffs. For three weeks following the James Madison loss, the Eagles had been on the edge of being left out in the cold for the second straight year.

Southern's foe in the first round would be Jackson State, the winner of the Southwestern Athletic Conference championship.

Jackson State had the top-rated defense in I-AA football against the run. Part of that was due to the fact the Tigers played in the pass-happy SWAC. But Jackson State also had the advantage of a huge defensive line— bigger than the lines of some National Football League teams.

But Vance Pike — a six-foot-four, 265 pounder who would end the season as a I-AA first team Kodak All-American — wasn't impressed; he'd already played against the best the Southeastern Conference could offer.

A high-school teammate of Jessie Jenkins and Larry West at Warner-Robins High, Pike was a big-time recruit and signed with Auburn.

But the "Loveliest Village on the Plain" didn't suit Pike at all. He was so disenchanted with the situation there that he left school following his freshman year. When West and Jenkins heard, they talked their former teammate into coming to GSC.

Pike, on the other hand, isn't much of a talker, but more the kind to lead by example. With him at one offensive tackle and Jeff Evans, a six-foot-five, 260-pound former defensive tackle, at the other offensive tackle, the Eagles' runners had very large holes to run through.

The night before the Jackson State game, Southern hosted a banquet at the Williams Center on campus. Russell told the troops to dress nicely. To Southern's players, that meant a shirt with a button-down collar and a clean pair of jeans.

Jackson State players walked into the Williams Center with some of the players wearing tuxedos. Their talk was just as flashy.

"Look at all the managers this team has," one Jackson State player said, referring to the lack of size on Southern's roster. Pointing at Southern's five-foot-eleven, 220-pound center, Jay Marshall, the Jackson State players feigned disbelief. "Hey, Jack, this is their center!"

At a pre-banquet speech, one of the speakers made a comment about how two great teams would play the next day. The Jackson State players snickered. As the teams sat down to dinner, some of the Tigers passed comments along with the potatoes.

"We're going to stomp on you little guys."

Though a few Southern players dished the talk right back, most of them ate their dinner and thought about how they'd have Jackson State eating its words.

It took the Eagles exactly 4:07 to take a lead they'd never lose. Not surprisingly, Jackson State quarterback Shannon Boyd came out throwing. After the Tigers were forced to punt at their own twenty-six on the first series, they got a break — a new first down — when Southern was called for unsportsmanlike conduct. Boyd went long on the first play, hoping to catch the Eagles down. He didn't. Chris Aiken made a strong move for the ball and intercepted it at his own eleven.

Ham showed JSU what it was in for early. His first play from scrimmage was a simple rollout . . . for forty-three yards. Two plays later, he found Tony Belser for a forty-eight-yard touchdown pass.

The Tigers never recovered as the Eagles played their most inspired defense of the season, intercepting Boyd four times, picking up two fumbles and holding JSU to 105 yards on the ground. Southern's defensive line actually used its size disadvantage as a plus; by employing better technique and by moving more quickly, they frustrated Jackson State.

Jenkins summed it up best: "Those guys were big. You've got to figure if a player is that big and not playing Division I, they can't be that good. I loved playing against those type of players. It was a lot easier to get by them because they were slow."

With the win over Jackson State, Southern was faced with a classic good news-bad news scenario. The good news was the Eagles would get to keep on playing. The bad news was the opponent would be Middle Tennessee State, which, after beating GSC 35-10 earlier in the season, had rolled over everyone else as well. The Blue Raiders were 11-0 and the top-ranked team in the country. Southern, in its first year in the playoffs, would have to beat MTSU in Murfreesboro — on artificial turf — to advance. In four earlier tries on rugs, Southern had failed.

But MTSU had its own problem — overconfidence. Blue Raider head coach Boots Donnelly was perturbed at his team's lackluster practices in the week prior to the game. He was concerned his team was taking the game too lightly.

All Russell had to worry about was keeping his team on the ground. . . literally. Post-season play was new to the Eagles, and so was flying. With the NCAA footing the bill for travel expenses, the Eagles would take a plane to their destination for the first time. For some of the GSC players, it was their first plane ride ever.

Mike Healey, a study in sideline concentration

Not Ham, though. When he was in the eleventh grade, he flew to the Bahamas and back as part of a school program. He slept the entire way home. He brought that same cool head to the game with MTSU. Though Ham had to relish the chance to clear the slate with Middle Tennessee and especially with Blue Raider quarterback Marvin Collier, he wouldn't say anything for the Blue Raiders to post in their locker room. Donnelly, for his part, kept Collier quiet by forbidding him to talk to the press the week before the game.

All Ham would do was profess his confi-

Diving into 'beautiful Eagle Creek' has become a tradition at Southern; it started with the first team in 1981

dence that Southern could win. He knew he'd missed some key reads in the earlier loss and could do better.

"They're a good team but we can beat them. We've been playing some teams that are as good as Middle Tennessee, but none were as well-coached."

The day before the game, the Eagles had to wait for two and a half hours at the Butler Aviation terminal in the Savannah Airport. The same plane that had been chartered to take Eastern Washington to its playoff game with Northern Iowa was Southern's chariot as well. On the earlier run, the pilots had detected a fuel run and the Eagles had to wait for it to be repaired.

Upon landing in Murfreesboro, it was clear that the weather would not be to Southern's advantage. It was bitterly cold. GSC's players were nervous but intense. This was a long way from playing the Jacksonville, Florida, police force team.

Middle Tennessee State had all that tradition on its side. In the Blue Raider room behind Johnny Red Floyd stadium were photographs of great Middle Tennessee State games through history, including many against archrival Tennessee Tech.

Southern's traditions were much more recent.

Russell told the Eagles that they'd have to treat the Blue Raiders the same as any other team. Just stick to the basics. As Russell would often say, "Repeat the things that make you successful."

Defensive line coach John Pate was doing that, getting his players fired up the same way he usually did, by slapping helmets. As usual, John Richardson stayed away from the helmet bashing by hiding behind Larry Boone.

"Coach Pate was like a little Coach Russell," Richardson said. "He would always refer to the fact that he wasn't big enough to play big-time college football. He just wanted to be one of the guys."

Pate did indeed have a lot in common with Russell. He first met Russell at a scrimmage game between Fort Benning and Southern in 1981. GSC won, 33-26, and Pate, the defensive coordinator at Fort Benning, was intrigued by Russell.

The following year, Pate got out of the Army and became an assistant at Georgia Southwestern, a team just starting its football program. After two years at Georgia Southwestern, he became the head coach at Union College in Barbourville, Kentucky, restarting a football program that had been dormant since World War II. But the grand experiment lasted only one year.

"I didn't get along with an administrator," Pate said. "It was a lady who had been there forty years. At a small school like that, if you don't get along with somebody, it's trouble. We got the football team off the ground, but we were terrible. It was a long year."

At the end of the season, Pate called Russell. As fate would have it, Russell had a few assistants moving on and had an opening on his staff.

For the Middle Tennessee State game, Pate made a few changes that proved to be important. He moved Eddie Johns, a six-foot-three, 275-pound defensive guard, to tackle, giving Southern a big defensive line with an emphasis on pass rushing. "We just felt confident we weren't going to let their little quarterback roll out on us," Pate said. "I thought we could put some pressure on him."

"We were ready to face the challenge at the time," said GSC wide receiver Monty Sharpe. "Everybody came out really pumped up before the game started. Throughout the years, we had been told we could not compete at this level. It just came to a point where we had gotten better and better each game. That's mainly what happened. You could see the intense look on each person's face. Everybody was of one accord."

The Blue Raiders opened up the first quarter the way they'd done in two previous meetings with the Eagles — by marching steadily down the field. MTSU had been extremely methodical and error-free in its 35-10 victory over Southern earlier in the season. This time, however, the Blue Raiders proved more human. Eagle linebacker Charles Carper finally stopped the advance with a well-timed hit on tailback Gerald Anderson that caused Anderson to fumble at the GSC twenty-nine, and linebacker Danny Durham scooped it up.

Southern scored quickly. After Ham found Monty Sharpe for an eighteen-yard pass, Gerald Harris ran six straight plays to the MTSU nine. Ham faked another handoff to Harris but tucked the ball low and went around right end for the score.

Middle Tennessee probably could have taken advantage of Johns' playing at tackle by running more plays to the outside, but the Raiders didn't. Instead, Johns broke the game open by shutting Collier's mouth. Three plays into Middle Tennessee's next possession, Johns, nicknamed "Wide Load," got on the outside shoulder of the lineman in front of him and slipped past him. Johns came up on Collier like a truck, blind-siding him to cause a fumble. Richardson picked it up and ran to the MTSU five. Harris ran twice to score, giving GSC back-to-back touchdowns in a minute. Collier was shaken up on the play and it may have affected him the rest of the game.

Harris continued his workhorse ethic on Southern's next drive, scoring from six yards out after pacing a thirteen-play, ninety-yard drive. Suddenly, Southern was up 21-0 and the Johnny Red Floyd Stadium crowd of 9,500 was quiet.

Eagles David Hodge (5), Robert Underwood (34) and Jessie

74

Jenkins (67) pursue MTSU quarterback Marvin Collier

Then came the scary part. With MTSU trailing by so much, the Blue Raiders would go to the air, hoping to find a hole in Southern's secondary. To have a reasonable chance, Middle Tennessee State had to get something going before halftime.

Cornerback Nay Young had gone into the season as Southern's top defensive back, so during the year, most opponents didn't take the risk of throwing his way. A speedy all-around athlete, he would often steal second and third in American Legion baseball games.

So instead of trying out Young, opposing quarterbacks usually elected to test Chris Aiken, who was a transfer from Chowan (North Carolina) Community College. Aiken went into the game with a team-leading eight interceptions to only four for Young, who was chafing at the bit to prove how good he was.

With Southern getting a good rush on Collier, the redshirt freshman quarterback couldn't be choosy when he threw. He had the bruises to remind him of Johns. With time running out in the second quarter, Collier threw a twenty-six-yard pass to Robert Alford. MTSU fullback Tony Burse followed the play with a twenty-one-yard romp to Southern's nineteen. Only seconds remained before intermission when Collier went for broke again. Young made what could have been a costly error by not watching Collier's eyes. Instead, Young was looking at the MTSU receiver, who had him beaten by a step. But the ball was under-thrown and Young made a diving interception in the end zone to preserve the halftime shutout.

MTSU was not a team to give up easily, however. On GSC's first series of the second half, Ham fumbled while cocking his arm to throw, and Blue Raider defender Bob Moorehead recovered the ball and ran it to Southern's ten-yard line. Two plays later, MTSU

tailback Dwight Stone ran it in from the five. Following the point after, Southern's lead was cut to 21-7.

Another Ham fumble set up another Middle Tennessee touchdown. Following a long drive by GSC, Ham lost the ball at the fourteen-yard line. Collier drove the Blue Raiders the remaining eighty-six yards and capped the drive with a pass that Ray Palhegyi leaped to grab for a twenty-one-yard touchdown at the end of the third quarter.

Southern's lead was only 21-14. MTSU was back in the game and so was the Johnny Red Floyd crowd, which began stomping its feet. Once Middle Tennessee got the ball back, it

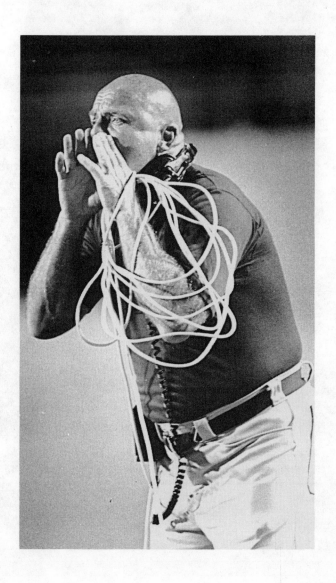

drove to Southern's twenty-four. Remembering his sandlot days, Young was about to complete another double steal. He was going to take the tight end, but at the last minute safety Brad Bowen switched with Young, allowing Young to take the flanker, Mike Pittman. Under a heavy rush, Collier threw a rainbow-like pass towards Pittman. Young and Pittman both went up for the ball. Young came down with it in the end zone.

Ham would make no more fumbles. He engineered an eighty-yard drive in twelve plays and Gerald Harris went over the top from the one to give the Eagles a 28-14 lead. It was Harris' third touchdown of the day. On thirty carries, he rushed for 148 yards.

But MTSU came back to score on a fourteen-yard run by Stone. This time, however, only 4:47 remained and Ham worked the clock as well as he did when he worked for a Statesboro meat-packing plant the summer of his freshman year. He never let the Blue Raiders get the ball back. MTSU had only one chance to stop Southern — on a third-and-two play. The Blue Raiders came with a very heavy rush, but Ham tossed to the closest familiar jersey, finding Herman Barron for an eleven-yard pass. The Eagles ran out the clock for sweet victory.

Two days earlier, some of the Eagles had taken their first plane ride. In a few days, some would get their first taste of snow. Southern would travel to Northern Iowa for a chance at the title game.

11 | '38 Trap Option' Puts Panthers On Ice

Donnie Allen (61) makes a tackle on the crucial final drive by Northern Iowa

Northern Iowa had advanced to the semifinal game with a 17-14 win over Eastern Washington, holding their opponent to only fifty-five yards on the ground. Over the course of the year, the Purple Panthers had allowed an average of only eighty-nine yards a game rushing. But they hadn't seen an option offense like Southern's.

Likewise, GSC hadn't faced a club that was as pass happy as UNI. The Panthers' quarterback, Mike Smith, had thrown for 2,579 yards and seventeen touchdowns. UNI could run as well, however, with fullback Carl Boyd rushing for 1,104 yards.

There were other numbers about UNI that bothered Russell even more. Northern Iowa played in the UNI-Dome, and the noise that 16,400 fans could generate could be intimidating.

The week before the game, Erk tried to prepare his team for the UNI-Dome by dragging them into Hanner Fieldhouse, cranking up the volume on a crowd noise tape and then having them run plays.

Panther coach Darrell Mudra, known as something of an eccentric for his style of coaching from the press box, tried to ready his team for Southern by bringing in a high-school quarterback who was familiar with the option to run plays against his defense.

The game would be televised live by Savannah station WJCL, with Georgia Southern putting together a network of stations in Macon, Atlanta and Columbus. WJCL had carried the only other live broadcast of a GSC football game — when the Eagles hosted Presbyterian in 1983 in Savannah's Memorial Stadium. This time, the game being televised meant a great deal more. Southern would even have Larry Munson, the voice of the Georgia Bulldogs, along to do color commentary.

Scouting for any game is important. In this case, some pre-game information Georgia Southern learned about Northern Iowa proved very enlightening. The Purple Panthers were confident of winning. So confident, in fact,

they'd already booked a plane to Tacoma, Washington, the following week. Tacoma would be the site of the I-AA championship game. To add insult to injury, the UNI-Dome officials greased the goalposts — so as to prevent Northern Iowa's euphoric fans from tearing them down after the Panthers' victory.

Southern's trip to Northern Iowa was uneventful. The Eagles landed at the airport at Waterloo, the town next door to Cedar Falls. The first thing some of the players did upon disembarking was get in a snowball fight, but the snow wasn't damp enough for good packing. The temperature was unbelievably cold; the wind-chill factor was fifteen below zero. The area had been hit by heavy snowfalls earlier than usual, but this type of weather wasn't new to the area and vehicles came well-equipped to drive in snow.

Russell had been concerned about how his players would feel so far from home. A little psychology was in order. Russell had spoken often and passionately of a little drainage ditch beside the team's practice fields. He called the ditch, in a wonderful euphemism, "Beautiful Eagle Creek." Before leaving for Iowa, he took a plastic milk jug and filled it with the gnat-infested waters from the ditch.

The jug traveled on the same plane with the players, and when the Eagles worked out in the UNI-Dome the day before the game, Russell called them together, told them he'd brought something special from home and ceremoniously sprinkled the contents of the jug over both end zones to keep the Purple Panthers from scoring and to help the Eagles. He also dabbed a little water on various parts of the field, saying things like, "This is where we'll stop them, at the thirty-four-yard line." With all the advantages UNI seemed to have, the Eagles were probably hoping for a little magic.

The day of the game, Southern stuck to its rituals. Repeat the things that make you successful. Russell had drilled that phrase into their minds so constantly that they did it without asking questions.

The pre-game stretch and head-butting circle some of the players did outside the locker room before games was fine in the South Georgia heat. But this was December in Iowa. No matter. The linemen bundled up in coats and trudged out of the UNI-Dome and into the snow. While early-arriving spectators inside the UNI-Dome gawked and pointed, the Eagles stuck to tradition.

John Richardson (77) and Hugo Rossignol (28)
assist Robert Underwood with another tackle

As things turned out, both defensive lines would have been better off stretching a little more, for they would get a lot of work. The Eagles' option clearly confused UNI early. On GSC's first drive, Ham ran for eleven yards and ten yards before handing off to Gerald Harris.

Harris, called "Mr. Touchdowns" for his ability in short yardage situations, was built low to the ground and had powerful legs. The whole season, he'd lost only five yards on the ground. Somehow, glory had always escaped him, though.

A Swainsboro High graduate, he had things lined up so he could walk on at the University of South Carolina with a chance at a scholarship. Following the 1982 season, however, Gamecock head coach Richard Bell, who had issued the invitation, was replaced by Joe Morrison. Harris did not want to go to Georgia Southern. It was too close and too small. But with his options at South Carolina drying up, Statesboro was looking better and better.

Russell told Harris he could come to practice as a walk-on with a chance of a scholarship. Before half the season was over, Harris had earned a partial scholarship and by the next season he had a full one.

While he always scored his share of touchdowns, he had never had a long run — his fifty-two-yard romp at South Carolina State was his first run ever over thirty-two yards. The plays he ran, mostly goal line or short yardage situations, meant he would have to run up the middle through the heart of defenses.

But Harris was nothing if not patient. A math major, he knew the more times he carried the ball, the better the odds were he'd break one.

On Southern's first series at UNI, it happened. Harris was supposed to run a routine off-tackle play, behind the blocking of Charles Carper and Jeff Evans. But when he broke past the line, there was a large hole. He saw most of the defensive players to the left, so he made a sharp cut to the right and down the sideline, outrunning three defenders to the corner of the end zone for a seventy-one-yard touchdown. Suddenly the noise at the UNI-Dome wasn't such a factor.

But UNI moved the ball just as easily and Boyd answered Harris with a sixteen-yard run for a touchdown.

In the newspapers the week of the game, UNI defensive back Moses Aimable, who also anchored the school's 4x400-meter relay squad, said how much he was looking forward to the game because Southern didn't have much of a passing attack. He said it would be like a vacation.

But Aimable didn't count on Monty Sharpe.

Sharpe, whose cousin, Sterling Sharpe, is the University of South Carolina's all-time leading receiver, was used to being over-looked. When he played at Reidsville High School, he hadn't even been recruited much by Southern. While GSC coaches had been around, it was usually to look at linebacker Warnell Anthony, a high-school teammate of Sharpe's.

Sharpe had just about resigned himself to going into the Navy following high school. He'd already taken the tests and even had thought about what type of job he'd like in the service when Southern coach Doc Spurgeon asked Sharpe if he'd like to play football.

While Sharpe wasn't a starter his freshman year, by his sophomore year he'd established himself as GSC's leading deep threat. He wasn't as fast as Aimable, but he had been clocked at sub-4.4 times in the forty-yard dash. By the time of the UNI game, Sharpe had already caught thirteen touchdown passes in his career — a GSC record.

Northern Iowa used man-to-man coverage in the secondary, and Aimable would not respect Sharpe. Instead of giving Sharpe a drop of five yards, Aimable stayed on him from the line of scrimmage.

"I knew he was fast and I was thinking, 'There's no way in the world I'll get by this guy,'" Sharpe said of Aimable. "He was so cocky that he wasn't backing up at all."

Midway through the first quarter, Ham gave Sharpe a choice of two patterns to run: an eighteen-yard curl pattern or a fly pattern. When Sharpe began running his route, Aimable tried to stay with him step for step. At fifteen yards into his pattern, however, Sharpe turned on the afterburners.

"I looked back and he was seven to ten yards behind," Sharpe said. "I said, 'Man, I'm going to score.' I had to stretch and the ball caught my fingertips. I looked back and he was gaining on me. There was no way I was going to let him catch me. I was five yards deep in the end zone when he pushed me from behind. I was too tired at the time to complain."

The reception put Southern up by seven points, but it also changed the complexion of the game. Suddenly UNI had to worry about the deep passing threat, which opened up Southern's running game.

Soon the game took on the semblance of a track meet. Smith tied the score a few moments later with an eleven-yard pass across the middle to Scott Francke. It was 14-14 and there was still 1:22 left in the first quarter. Three minutes later, Southern's drive stalled and Foley nailed a thirty-five-yard field goal. UNI answered with a field goal of its own; Kevin Mote hit a forty-yarder to tie the score at seventeen after Scott Owens dropped a pass for the Panthers in the end zone. Another Mote field goal, this one of twenty-two yards, put Northern Iowa up 20-17.

Mote's second field goal came with only forty-eight seconds left in the half. At intermission, it was obvious the Eagles were getting beat at the line of scrimmage. Northern Iowa had more yards rushing and passing and twenty first downs to eight for Southern. Boyd had 122 yards by himself.

GSC didn't wait long to change the momentum in the second half. On Southern's first drive, Ham ran for two straight downs to the UNI thirty-nine. After another seven-yard run by Ham, Ricky Harris took a pitchout, shook off Tim Moses on the corner and heard the end zone calling his name for a thirty-two-yard touchdown.

After both teams punted to break up the scoring parade, UNI marched from its thirteen to GSC's six. Smith tried to find

Francke again, but Nay Young was waiting this time to break up the pass on third down. On fourth down, Mote hit a twenty-three-yard field goal to cut Southern's lead to 24-23.

After Southern stalled, Mote connected again to give his team a 26-24 lead eight seconds into the final quarter. Another UNI drive was broken up at the eight when safety Brad Bowen intercepted Smith's pass. Less than two minutes later, Gerald Harris ran off tackle for thirteen yards and another score. Ricky Harris attempted a two-point conversion but was stopped, so the Eagles had a

Gerald Harris, a walk-on who became a national record holder

30-26 lead. Foley made it 33-26 on a twenty-nine-yard field goal with 7:14 left.

UNI tailback Carl Boyd tied the score at thirty-three with a three-yard run with 2:44 left.

After engineering two close wins in the past three games, Tracy Ham was ready to do it again. Starting from the twenty-three, Gerald Harris led the Eagles with runs of nineteen, thirteen and eight yards. Ricky Harris added a sixteen-yard run to get the Eagles to the thirty-four. But time was running out. Southern had less than a minute left. Offensive coordinator Paul Johnson sent in the play — "38 trap option."

Ham tried to read UNI's defense. When he saw a Panther linebacker commit inside, he took it outside for a twenty-one-yard touchdown to put Southern on top for good, 39-33, with only thirty-four seconds left. Foley's point-after made it 40-33 and Southern had to hold on again.

Smith naturally went deep, but Young came up with an interception with seventeen seconds left to seal the win.

Somehow, the dream of Jenkins and every other GSC player now had a chance to come true.

Russell couldn't wipe the smile off his face. "Being up here, with all the snow and things to see, I felt like I was in a dream all day," he said. "We're going to get back on a plane and get back to Georgia — where it's warm."

Georgia Southern had a date with Furman for the I-AA national championship. Ironically, two teams separated by less than two hundred miles would travel three thousand miles across the country for the title game. The year before, the championship game had been in Charleston, but that city had asked out of its agreement to host the champion-

Tim Foley (9) kicked two field goals and three extra points in the victory over Northern Iowa

ship game before the 1985 season.

Faced with only a handful of possible sites, the NCAA chose Tacoma because it was the only city with the proper facilities to show much interest in hosting the game. The NCAA bought time on ESPN for the game to be broadcast. In south Georgia, television stations WJCL in Savannah and WTGS in Hardeeville would also broadcast the contest.

The week of practice before the Furman game was brief. Unlike Northern Iowa, the Eagles knew a little bit about Furman, and much of it was tinged with envy.

The Paladins represented the class of I-AA football, while the Eagles were surely the upstarts. Furman had won the Southern Conference in five of the past six years and had sent twenty-seven players on to professional football. In 1983, the Paladins advanced to the semifinals of the I-AA playoffs. Unlike Southern, which divided forty-nine scholarships among its players, Furman had the full limit of seventy scholarships allotted to I-AA teams.

Furman also had thirty-one Georgia players on its roster. But unlike GSC, most of the Georgians on the Paladins' roster were from established football programs around affluent Metro Atlanta suburbs — whereas Southern relied on players from smaller rural towns in southern Georgia. Academically, Furman also had more snob appeal. Its alumni often referred to Harvard as "the Furman of the North."

With the end of the season only a week away, Russell didn't want to get any of his players hurt. But the Eagles were too fired up to take it easy in practice. On Tuesday before

84

the game, rover Hugo Rossignol and corner-back Nay Young, both going after a pass, collided and went down. Young was unhurt and Rossignol was fortunate to come out of the incident only with a bruised shoulder. Somehow, kickoff specialist Trey Herold bruised a shin in the practice as well.

Wednesday would be the Eagles' last official day of practice. At the end of the workouts, Statesboro mayor Thurman Lanier spoke, as did GSC president Dale Lick. Along with a wooden replica of an Eagle, Russell was presented with two official "Eagle Creek" water jugs.

Erk had his team's freshmen carry the seven seniors off the field on their shoulders. There was some concern the freshmen would dump the seniors into Eagle Creek, but the seniors took care of that worry by baptizing themselves.

When Russell boarded the plane to Tacoma from Savannah the next morning, he didn't bring the new jugs. He stuck to the old milk jug he'd used before. Remember — repeat the things that make you successful.

The plane ride was a wild one. Players, boosters and press were all on the same plane. But by the time the plane landed that evening, the mood was much more subdued. A heavy fog blanketed the Tacoma area and the plane was forced to make an alternate landing at Boeing Field, north of Seattle-Tacoma airport. After what seemed like an eternity, the team was greeted by buses which would take them to the team's hotel in Fife.

On the ground, the fog was just as thick as it had looked from the sky. The majestic Mount Rainier was nowhere to be seen. Even the Tacoma Dome, which was just off the interstate, was difficult to see through the fog.

Deep down, Russell had to be smiling. At least he didn't have to worry about his team's being distracted by sightseeing.

As soon as the buses rolled into the hotel, the players grabbed a quick bite to eat at a buffet table and then were hustled off to the Tacoma Dome for practice. Their last one.

12 | *A Miracle Comeback, A National Title*

Erk told his team, 'There ain't no tomorrow,' and they listened

If Furman's players felt superior to Southern's, they were too classy to show it. Unlike some of Southern's other opponents, the Paladins refused to talk down the Eagles. Head coach Dick Sheridan, now at North Carolina State, had prepared his squad well to stop GSC's option. By bringing free safety Steve Squire up to the line, Sheridan would have one man to take the pitch, another man to watch Tracy Ham and another to go man-to-man with the fullback to stop the dive.

All season long, Russell had said his team may as well pack things up if a team was able to stop Southern's option. But the Eagles may have been a lot more flexible than he'd let on.

Secretly, Southern's players looked at Furman and thought they had a good chance. Unlike most of GSC's opponents, Furman was actually smaller than Georgia Southern. Nobody on Furman's offensive or defensive line weighed more than 230 pounds. What the Eagles didn't know was the Paladins were just as quick and well-schooled in technique as GSC was.

Donnie Allen, a 5-11, 250-pound defensive guard, remembers the Eagles as maybe being a little overconfident.

"All year long, we had been playing teams that were bigger than we were. We always said, if we do this against bigger teams, wait until we get a team our size. Before the game, things were really calm. I think we might have been a little overconfident."

Allen had played his high school football at Suwanee High School in Like Oak, Florida, about forty-five miles away from Ham's high school of Alachua-Santa Fe. GSC assistant coach Mike Healey first spotted Donnie Allen when the latter was wrestling at a regional tournament.

Healey was actually recruiting another wrestler-football player who would wind up going to Auburn. Although Allen beat the wrestler in the finals, he didn't hear from Healey until the homecoming game the following season. Southern was looking for a big, bruising fullback, and Allen certainly fit

the bill.

Except that when he came to GSC, he was moved to defense. Before the championship game was over, though, it was his running ability that would come in handy.

Furman had to punt on its first possession. Worried about having a nervous returner dropping the punt, Russell set up no return and Southern had to settle for the ball at its own thirteen.

It looked like a mistake, but with Ham, field position isn't that important. Gerald Harris broke a tackle to go for an eleven-yard first down to the thirty-seven. Two plays later, Ham threw deep over the middle for Monty Sharpe, who with the aid of Ham's hard throw was able to beat strong safety Russell Rush for a thirty-eight-yard gain to Furman's thirty-one-yard line. Gerald Harris broke another tackle to go fifteen yards to the sixteen. Two plays later, Southern was at third-and-three when Ham, with a defender hanging on him, was forced to throw the ball away.

No problem — Southern could count on Tim Foley. But the angle from twenty-seven yards out was difficult and Foley was nervous. The sophomore kicker pushed it wide to the right.

Then Bobby Lamb took over. The No. 3 quarterback in passing efficiency among Division I-A or I-AA players, Lamb was called "Atari" by his coaches for his computer-like ability to pick apart opponents. Though he wasn't the runner Ham was, Lamb spurred his team's drive by running twice — once for a first down and the other time for six yards. But it was tailback John Bagwell who put Furman on top, running for eight yards and then using a block from Kenneth Goldsmith for a one-yard touchdown run with 2:54 left in the first quarter.

Again, Ham was able to move the ball,

but the Paladins stopped him from finding the end zone. Stymied at the Furman twenty-six when his pass was batted down by defensive end Jeff Blankenship, Southern settled for a forty-four-yard field goal by Foley.

Southern was having trouble developing a rush on Lamb. Led by center Gene Reeder who, at only 5-11 and 212 pounds, was named the Southern Conference's best blocker that season, Furman was trapping, slanting, doing everything it could to frustrate Southern's defense.

On second down and thirteen, the Eagles

Jessie Jenkins (67) led an inspired defense in the second half against Furman

knew Lamb would probably pass, so the blitz was on. Rossignol, who had already bloodied his nose a few plays earlier, came from one side and Danny Durham the other. Somehow Lamb got free long enough to find Chris Speaks, a former quarterback, for a twenty-seven-yard pass to Southern's twenty-one-yard line. Two plays later, GSC was called for defensive holding, giving Furman the ball at the Eagles' nine. With fullback John Drye clobbering Durham with a block, Bagwell scored his second touchdown from the nine.

Defensively, the Paladins started to zero in on stopping the option, and that caused Southern to make mistakes. On third down and three, offensive tackle Jeff Evans stood up too soon and the Eagles lost five yards for illegal procedure. Faced with a third-and-eight, Ham found Belser with a twenty-five-yard pass. Three plays later, the Eagles had gotten nowhere on the ground, so Ham tossed it to Belser again for eighteen yards.

Three plays later on third and three, Gerald Harris was stopped short of a first down and Foley came in and hit a thirty-three-yard field goal.

Lamb continued to frustrate Southern. He passed for eight yards to Kirk Burnett, seventeen to Speaks, nine to Bagwell and twenty to Larry Grady. A pass interference call against Southern brought Lamb to Southern's ten, where he ran a bootleg right for a score. This time, Drye flattened Nay Young on the block and Furman was up 21-6 with fifty-six seconds left in the first half.

The Eagles were in trouble, and offensive coordinator Paul Johnson knew it. The moment Russell had fretted about — the day somebody would stop his option — had come. Actually, the Paladins hadn't completely shut down Southern's option but had frustrated it, and by taking a big lead, the Paladins were forcing GSC into a passing situation.

To the Eagles' credit, nobody's head was bowed at halftime. Something was wrong, but the Eagles had been in tough spots before. Johnson told Southern's offense it simply wasn't executing. Tracy Ham told Johnson the Eagles would win the game.

"We didn't make that many adjustments," Johnson said. "We were going to use the same passing routes we had used all season. We just hadn't had to pass that much all year."

Russell challenged his troops. "They are not beating us," he said. "We are beating ourselves."

He told his defense it needed to stop Furman a few times to give the Eagles' offense a chance, adding that eventually Southern would put some points on the board. Going off the field at halftime, Ham had told Allen the same thing.

But before the situation could get better, it got worse. The new plan of attack got off to a rough start as Ham's blind pitch to Ricky Harris was off the mark and, in a hurry to pick it up, Harris kicked it out of bounds for a fifteen-yard loss. Ham then overthrew Gerald Harris on a screen pass on third and twenty-two and Southern was forced to punt.

Furman wasted little time in scoring. Brian Jager gained nine yards on a pitch from Lamb, and Goldsmith had gains of nine and nineteen yards to GSC's thirty-three-yard line. Instead of running again, Sheridan crossed up Southern by having Lamb pass. Furman's quarterback lobbed it over the middle to Larry Grady, who caught the ball, bounced off Young in a crowd and found his route open to the end zone for a thirty-three-yard touchdown catch. It was 28-6, and Southern's dream of a national title was very much in doubt.

Then, to the casual observer, Southern did something strange. In a passing situation, the Eagles took out Ricky Harris, the team's leading receiver, and put in Frank Johnson.

Russell had noticed that Harris wasn't running very well, and Paul Johnson wanted his namesake in there because he thought he was a better receiver than Harris.

"I was kind of nervous at that point, but I fell on my knees and said my prayers," Johnson said. He tried to remember what receivers coach Jay Russell had taught him: "Bob your head like a duck and track the ball into your hands."

Ham left little time for second-guessing. On the first play from scrimmage, he hit Johnson for a screen pass and the freshman walk-on from Sylvania traveled twenty-five yards. Ham passed again to Johnson for four yards and then pitched to Johnson for two yards. On third and four, Ham dropped back to pass again, but was pressured. He broke two tackles and gained twelve yards to Furman's thirty-five.

After Monty Sharpe dropped a Ham pass and after a delay-of-game penalty, things were getting difficult for Ham. On third down and fifteen, he threw with a man on his back for no gain to Johnson. After a pass to Gerald Harris went back fifteen yards for a clipping penalty, Southern was faced with a third down and twenty-one.

Then, for the first time, Furman made an obvious mistake. Knowing Ham had to pass, the Paladins rushed just two men as the rest

Southern fans cheered in disbelief as their Eagles overcame a 22-point deficit

of the defense tried to cut off the passing routes. But given plenty of time, Ham found Tony Belser for a twenty-two-yard pass play. Then Ham went for the kill. On first down at the Furman twenty-four, he rifled the ball to Sharpe, who waltzed into the end zone. With seven minutes left in the third quarter, the Eagles had scored their first touchdown. Ham ran in for a two-point conversion to cut Furman's lead to 28-14.

Inspired, GSC's defenders turned aggressive. By bringing up the cornerbacks tighter and dropping the linebackers a little deeper, Southern hoped to stop Furman's mid-range passing attack. Twice, Allen rushed hard to force Lamb to hurry his passes. On third and eight, Lamb tried to get it to Kirk Burnett, but Young knocked it down.

An average punt travels seventy miles per hour and has more than six hundred revolu-

tions per minute, but Paladin punter Alston Hamilton didn't reach those standards as his punt went only twenty-eight yards to give Southern excellent field position at its own forty-four.

On second down, Ham found Herman Barron on a quick out pattern for a sixteen-yard gain. Two plays later, Ham went over the middle to Frankie Johnson, who had a defender on either side of him. Johnson ducked low, the defenders collided, and he caught the pass and ran it in for a forty-yard touchdown.

In less than six minutes, the Eagles were back in the game and had the momentum. Again, GSC's defense took over. After Lamb was rushed heavily, he threw two straight incomplete passes, and Hamilton had to punt again.

Instead of continuing to pass, the coaches

Frank Johnson (48) goes high to make THE catch against Furman . . .

felt they had opened things up enough to use the more reliable option. Ham dropped back to pass but scrambled out of the pocket for twelve yards before Blankenship grabbed him by the ankles. On the next play, Ham pitched on the left flat to Gerald Harris, who had only one defensive man in front of him. GSC receiver Darren Chandler made a perfect block on linebacker Verdell Patterson, and Harris outran cornerback Jerome Norris for a fifty-two-yard touchdown. Foley's point-after tied the game at twenty-eight with 2:28 left in the third quarter.

Reeling, Furman tried to regroup by running the ball instead of passing, but they got nowhere. On third down and one, Bagwell was stopped for no gain by linebackers Danny Durham and Robert Underwood.

. . . while the referee signals touchdown and Furman players look on in amazement

93

After a five-yard run by Gerald Harris, Ham made a quick move to avoid two defenders and wound up with five yards for a first down. Everything that wasn't working for Southern earlier began to fall into place. Ham found Johnson for a thirteen-yard pass completion, then pitched to Ricky Harris for fourteen yards and another first down. Harris then caught an eleven-yard spiral from Ham to the Furman twelve. Southern's offensive line gave Ham plenty of time to throw one more time. He pump faked once before finding Herman Barron open in front of the end zone, and Barron strutted in to put Southern up 35-28.

A lesser team, after blowing such a big lead, might have folded at that point, but not Furman. Sheridan was smart enough to figure out Southern had devised a way to stop the medium-range passes Lamb had done so well with earlier, so Furman went back to its option attack.

The Paladins' first play was a pitch from Lamb to Jager for nineteen yards, with Drye making a key block on Durham. One play later, Lamb hesitated long enough to commit Durham and pitched again to Jager, this time for ten yards to the right side. Lamb ran fourteen yards on the other side to GSC's thirty-one. Four more carries followed until the Paladins were at Georgia Southern's seven. With Goldsmith leading the blocking and plowing under Nay Young, Bagwell scored around the left side with 7:58 remaining in the game. Esval's point-after tied the game at 35-35.

On GSC's next possession, Ham drove to the GSC forty-one before he was forced out of bounds. He got up limping, favoring his left leg, but showed he was all right one play later when he scrambled for four yards. With the ball at the GSC forty-seven, the Eagles were short of the first down by inches. Russell chose to gamble and Ham was able to

Jubilant teammates mob Frank Johnson in the end zone

94

sneak for two yards and a first down. It may have been the biggest play of the game.

A quick release allowed Ham to find Delano Little for a twenty-six-yard pass play to the Furman twenty-five. After Gerald Harris gained three yards, however, Furman pressured Ham into two bad throws and Foley came in for a thirty-nine-yard field goal attempt.

Foley's kick was a low line drive that cleared the bar with inches to spare, and Southern took a 38-35 lead. Holder Monty Sharpe sprinted to the goal line in celebration as Foley watched the kick. Only 3:37 remained.

But that was enough time for Furman. Lamb engineered an eighty-yard drive in seven plays, locking up with Jager for a twenty-six-yard pass play, combining with Jager for eighteen yards on a lateral and then letting Bagwell (who else?) cut back to take it in from the four-yard line. Esval's point-after gave Furman a 42-38 lead with 1:32 left to play.

You could hear hearts pounding three thousand miles away in Statesboro. GSC had to score quickly, and a field goal obviously wouldn't do.

An Eagle holding penalty brought the ball back following the kickoff to the GSC eighteen. Only 1:17 remained. Ham struck quickly, however, tossing a long pass over the middle that Johnson was able to run under for a fifty-three-yard completion.

Ham carried for four yards to the Furman twenty-five and was able to get out of bounds to stop the clock with fifty-two seconds left. Ham dropped back to pass again, but Adrian Depres came up with Furman's first sack of the game for a five-yard loss. Forced to call a time out, GSC regrouped. Everyone in the Dome knew that Ham had to throw. He tried deep to the end zone but overthrew Monty

Sharpe in the process.

The clock seemed to be striking twelve for the Cinderella team, when, with only thirty-eight seconds left, center Jay Marshall appeared to forget the snap count. Everybody on the line and the backfield moved except him. The only problem was, he was the guy with the ball. But wait. Furman was called for encroachment on the play, so on fourth and eleven, Southern got a second chance.

This time, the snap count was perfect, but the primary receiver, Monty Sharpe was covered. Ham settled for his secondary receiver, as Belser came back for a seventeen-yard reception with thirty-eight seconds left. Ham quickly threw the next pass away in Sharpe's direction to stop the clock. On the next play, Paladin linebacker Verdell Patterson broke through the line and Ham was forced to throw it away again to avoid a sack. Now only fourteen seconds remained. The dream was fading.

Just prior to Foley's field goal that had put Southern up 38-35 moments earlier, Johnson had called what he referred to as a "four-way stretch route." The last time the play was run, Squire, the free safety, had cheated towards the side Ham was rolling out to, which left Frank Johnson open, but Ham, under a heavy rush, didn't see Frank Johnson.

Paul Johnson called the play again with Frank Johnson in mind this time.

It is third down as Ham barks out the signals, almost in slow motion. Johnson is in the left flat, then crosses over towards the middle of the end zone. This time he is not as open. Strong safety Russell Rush is in front of him, Squire is cutting across and Norris is behind Johnson. Ham somehow fires a pass between the three as Johnson leaps for the ball and comes down with it in the end zone. The referee signals touchdown as Norris looks on in disbelief. The scoreboard reads "Ga. Southern 44, Furman 42", and only ten seconds remain.

The first person to Johnson is Gerald Harris, who falls on him. Jeff Evans is next in the celebration. Soon most of the Eagles are jumping up and down in the end zone.

The jubilation soon appeared premature, however. Foley's point-after was wide after a bad snap, and the Eagles' end zone celebration cost them a fifteen-yard unsportsmanlike conduct penalty, to be assessed on the kickoff. Furman would get two chances.

Mark Rudder nearly ended it on the ensuing kick-off as he ran thirty-six yards to GSC's twenty-five. Warnell Anthony, the hard-hitting grand dragon of Southern's KKK (Krazy Kick Koverage Unit) finally shoved Rudder out of bounds.

Still four seconds were left. Only three GSC defenders would rush on the final play; the rest would be defensive backs. One of the rushers, however, was Donnie Allen, the former fullback turned defensive guard. With receivers flooding the end zone, Allen chased down quarterback Lamb and forced his desperation pass to James Brown to fall short. Time had expired.

Pandemonium ensued. Eddie Johns and Hugo Rossignol sat in the middle of the field and tried to let it all sink in. In their second year of 1-AA competition, the Eagles had won the national championship. No school had ever done such a thing.

Waiting for the players back home after a long plane ride were fans at the airport, more fans at the field house.

The first question Tracy Ham was asked was, "What do you do for an encore?" But before the Eagles worried about the next year, they had to savor this one.

Eagle fans turned out by the thousands to welcome home their national champions

Next page: Chris Aiken (18) and Terry Young (30) share a 'high five' after beating Furman

13 | *A Stadium Worthy Of A Champion*

"Successful colleges will start laying plans for a new stadium; unsuccessful ones will start hunting for a new coach." — Will Rogers

When Allen E. Paulson was a high-school running guard and center for the Tomales High Braves in the farming community of Tomales, California, knee pads were not part of the usual equipment.

"They beat the beejesus out of my knees," he said. "They used to always submarine me and all those guys jumped on. I remember how banged up I used to get. You've got to be born a certain way to be a football player. You can't say, 'I want to go play football,' and get on the team. When I was in high school, I was six-foot, 180-pounds. Working out on a farm or a ranch, you get to be pretty strong."

While Paulson left prep football to go onto bigger and better things, the sport never left him. Georgia Southern's athletic program has been called "the most ambitious college program in the country" by the *Sporting News*. But ambition lacking the means to fulfill it is little more than wishful thinking. Without people like Paulson, M. C. Anderson, Morris Lupton, Glenn Bryant and other contributors,

GSC would still be dreaming about a stadium and undoubtedly about national championships.

Paulson, sixty-three, grew up in Clinton, Iowa, but left home at thirteen supporting himself by doing odd jobs, including selling newspapers and cleaning the lobby and restrooms of a hotel in Clinton. Two years later, he took a bus to California, where he worked on a farm and went to high school. After graduation, he went back to Iowa, attended Iowa State Teacher's College and continued his education in electrical engineering at West Virginia University. When World War II came along, he served in the Army. He returned home safely and was employed as a flight engineer for Trans World Airlines, starting at thirty cents an hour.

One of TWA's planes, the four-engine Lockheed Constellation, was frequently plagued by a drop in oil pressure, causing it to lose power. Paulson took out a $1,500 loan at TWA's credit union, bought a surplus Constellation engine and tinkered with it until he solved the problem with a valve. He offered the modification to TWA free, but the company rejected it. He went on to sell it to other airlines and eventually even to TWA,

What started as a giant mud pit was developed into Paulson Stadium, which has been called 'the prettiest little stadium in America'

starting his business career.

Today he is the chairman, president and chief executive officer of Gulfstream Aerospace Corporation in Savannah. It is the world's largest privately owned aircraft manufacturing company. According to a *Forbes* magazine article last fall, he is one of the four hundred wealthiest men in America.

The first real connection Paulson had with Georgia Southern came when he was asked to speak to GSC's electrical engineering department. That paved the way for a much greater request by Georgia Southern.

A stadium had been in the planning stages even before GSC enticed Erk Russell to Georgia Southern. When Statesboro businessman Jack Wilson cornered athletic director Bucky Wagner at a Rotary Club dinner and asked what could be done to help bring Russell to the school, Wagner told him, "Call him up and tell him you're the chairman of the stadium committee."

Glenn E. Bryant, at the time a state senator and a former mayor of Hinesville, donated $208,000 to purchase 55.2 acres of land northwest of the campus as a site for the new stadium.

Morris Lupton, founder of the Time Saver convenience stores and a Statesboro resident, donated up to $480,000 to construct a facilities building adjacent to the field to house locker rooms and a booster club entertainment room.

M. C. Anderson, who, like Paulson, is a rags-to-riches story, grew up in Bulloch County and, from one bulldozer in 1962, worked his business into one of the largest construction firms in the South. Anderson did all the initial preparations for the stadium, providing time, money and equipment, estimated at more than $435,000 worth. He also reminded GSC officials that Paulson would be a good person to contact for more

Allen Paulson presents an artist's rendering of the stadium which will bear his name

funds, which Southern sorely needed to finish the job.

"We needed to do something quickly," Wagner said. "We couldn't afford the payments at Womack Field. We couldn't draw a good enough crowd there to pay the expenses."

GSC officials estimated they needed $4.2 million to build the stadium. Counting on a $1.5 million revenue bond, the school would still be more than $1.6 million short.

Going on Anderson's suggestion, the school contacted Paulson. With the help of Bo Ginn, a Millen resident who was then a U.S. Representative and a candidate for gov-

101

ernor, GSC president Dale Lick and Wagner were able to set up a meeting with Paulson, where they offered a proposal. They explained the good a stadium would do for the college and the community. It was mentioned that the stadium would be named after Paulson if he made a significant contribution.

He did. More than $1 million worth.

"I tried to figure out what could I do to help the area that Gulfstream is involved in the most," Paulson said. "I concluded that Georgia Southern would be the one place that would mean more to more people than any other thing that I could give to. You can't give to everybody. You have to pick a favorite. But they do service this whole area. A lot of people in Savannah are interested in Georgia Southern sports. I think since the

stadium has been built, a lot of people in the area go to the games there."

But for all the high-minded goals, Paulson may not have donated if he hadn't been a football fan. Already a major contributor to the University of Georgia's athletic program, Paulson was twice honored by being named to coach the Bulldogs' varsity in games against UGA alumni players. He kids that he's the only undefeated football coach of a major college program.

As far as having his name on the stadium, that didn't matter to Paulson. But it did to his children, who, he said, would have screamed if his donation had been anonymous. Though seeing his name on the stadium isn't an "ego thing," he admits a twinge of pride at seeing it.

"Everybody wants to leave something permanent behind, do something that's lasting," Paulson said.

The only person possibly not happy about the situation was Anderson. Though he will not say it for the record, Anderson was reportedly miffed that he was snubbed when it came to naming the stadium. His secretary said the topic "is a very touchy one with him."

He'd actually been asked whether he wanted his name on the stadium, Wagner said, but had declined. That may have been just modesty. Nobody but Anderson knows for sure what he felt, but GSC officials say he expected that the school would have insisted his name be on the stadium in some fashion.

"M. C. Anderson is a leader and he's going

to be first in everything he does," Wagner said. "There are no second-place trophies in his house. He's as good a friend as we have. He's the one that got the stadium plans started."

Though Anderson does not attend the team's games, he still has connections to GSC football. His daughter married a former player, Robert Baker. And Jessie Jenkins, the last of the original Eagles, is now employed by Anderson as a pipe supervisor.

As the new stadium was being built, Southern's players couldn't wait. Nearly every day during construction, they'd take a trip over to the site. As the press box neared completion, the players would climb on top of its roof to get a better view of the surroundings.

"All the time we were playing in Womack Field, we felt the better we played, the better the facility would be," Eagle linebacker John Richardson said. "The first few teams had to show whether Southern would have a good football program."

Finally, on September 19, 1984, slightly more than four years after the school decided to restart its football program, Georgia Southern had a stadium to match its lofty ambitions. There was seating for eighteen thousand people with two expansion phases planned, eventually allowing the stadium to seat fifty thousand. There were also 5,200 parking spaces, a facility building with room for booster functions on the top floor and locker rooms underneath.

The Eagles christened the stadium with a 48-11 win over Liberty Baptist and since that time have lost only one game there. Something to do with pride.

Georgia Southern needed to call on its friends again before the start of the 1985 season. To help pay off the bond and make addi-

Major contributors M. C. Anderson (second from right) and Morris Lupton (right) with Bucky Wagner and Dale Lick

The 1983 GSU Eagles are addressed by Wagner at the site of the new stadium

tional improvements to the stadium and the athletic department, GSC needed $700,000. Once again Paulson came to the rescue, issuing the "Paulson Challenge." For every dollar raised by GSC's boosters, he'd match it — up to $350,000.

Opposite: Paulson dedicates stadium
Above: Erk presents a national championship ring to Mr. Paulson

Southern eventually raised the money. A national championship along the way didn't hurt the effort.

Attendance at Paulson Stadium doubled during the 1985 and '86 seasons

14 | A Marked Team— Everybody Wants A Piece

Erk Russell leaned back in the chair, folding his tanned arms across his muscular chest. On the wall behind him, a large white banner hung proclaiming, "Georgia Southern — 1985 NCAA National Champions." He glanced out the window of the Lupton Facilities Building where the sun beat down on a handful of fans on the field at Allen E. Paulson Stadium. It was picture day, and media and fans alike had gathered to meet the man and the players and rub elbows with last year's champions.

In front of Russell sat a handful of reporters, some equipped with TV cameras, others with tape recorders and some with notebooks.

"Ask me a question," belted Erk.

"What are your chances of repeating as national champions?" came the response.

"Y'all don't waste any time do you?" said Erk. He gazed out the window again where the crowd of fans began to swell in number. "We've got as much chance of winning the national championship this year as we did last year at this time — zero."

The reporters laughed. Erk has a knack for saying the right thing at the right time. More questions were asked and more answers fol-

lowed. Players began to arrive at the stadium. Some came by car, others by bus, and each would scramble for position in the shade against the wall of the homeside stands. It was a hot South Georgia August day, ninety-five degrees at least with air so thick it made breathing a chore. It was Erk's kind of day:

"Nothing better to practice in than a hot day in the black dirt with gnats buzzing in your ears. Gets you in shape. We may not be better than a lot of the teams we play, but we can sure be in better condition."

Fans gathered around the players throughout the afternoon taking pictures, collecting autographs and all asking about repeating as national champions.

"We'll give it our best shot," answered Tracy Ham.

"We've got to take them one game at a time," said Danny Durham.

I'm not thinking about a national championship," said Gerald Harris. "I'm thinking about the Florida Gators."

The Florida Gators. The college football world sat and wondered what Georgia Southern was doing playing that team. Just five years earlier, the Eagles had struggled with another team from the Sunshine State, but one less known than the Gators. That Magnum Force team consisted of members of the Jacksonville-Duval County Police Department. The Eagles won that game. Now bring on the Gators.

"It's the most important game we've played because it is the next one," said Erk.

Nothing about reliving the glory days he shared at the University of Georgia, when the Bulldogs played the Gators every year in an annual grudge match. Nothing about Georgia Southern getting the opportunity to play with the "big boys" of the Southeastern Conference. Nothing about David killing Goliath. It was simply the next game.

Erk preached it to his players. But despite the constant reminder from the man about Florida being just another game, it was hard for the champions of 1985 to think of anything else.

The University of Florida has one of the largest, if not the largest, press contingencies in the United States, and all of them wanted to talk to Tracy Ham. All of them wanted to know about this team from Statesboro. Just who are these guys, anyway?

Every day at practice, a handful of press people were on hand with cameras whirring, pencils scratching, noting every movement the Eagles made. It was a three-ring circus with Georgia Southern no longer being a side show, but finally playing under the big top.

The game itself wasn't the only thing attracting attention. Athletic Director Bucky Wagner was being interviewed for the AD job at Florida and was considered a leading candidate. Georgia Southern President, Dr. Dale Lick, was in the final days of his administration, with his final official duty scheduled to be attending the Georgia Southern-Florida game. And there was rumor of an NCAA investigation into the Georgia Southern football program.

They all caused distraction, but Erk kept preaching.

"It's important because it's the next one." And the players tried to listen. But the media circus whirled around them and concentration was difficult.

Wagner came to Georgia Southern as athletic director in 1980 and had taken a nondescript athletic department in severe financial trouble and put it on solid footing. There were grumblings, as is always the case in any business, yet Wagner stood firm on financial matters and as a result had earned the respect of his peers throughout the country. He applied for the athletic director's job at Florida not because he wanted to leave Georgia Southern but because he felt it a professional obligation to himself to pursue what looked to be a golden career opportunity. An athletic budget several million dollars larger than Georgia Southern's and a salary more than twice his current one would attract anyone in the athletic business.

Florida allotted 7,200 tickets to Georgia Southern for the game, and the Eagles faithful responded by buying every one of them. The Florida ticket office was surprised and so were the folks at Georgia Southern. In 1985, the Eagles had averaged slightly more than eight thousand customers per home game, and now they were selling more than seven thousand tickets to a game on the road.

T-shirts and sweatshirts sold quickly. Sports Buffs in the Statesboro Mall printed one with an Eagle riding an alligator with the words "Riding High on Gator Hide" emblazoned across the chest. The college bookstore was pressed to keep Eagle souvenirs on the shelves. Statesboro and Georgia Southern fans were working themselves into a frenzy over a football game.

And through all the distractions, Erk kept preaching.

"It's the most important game because it is the next one."

To Erk, that may have been the case, and maybe to the players also. But to the fans, it was the Eagles' shining moment in the bright sun of big-time football.

More T-shirts sold and fans searched for tickets as the frenzy of the town became more and more evident. People talked of nothing else. The *Statesboro Herald* ran a week-long series of articles about not only the game but all the peripheral activities. Gatherings at breakfast or lunch or dinner always turned their conversation to THE game.

"We've got a chance to win this thing."

"No way. *This is Florida.*"

"Tracy Ham can play with anybody. We can win it."

"Florida's bigger, stronger, faster and has more depth than we do. There just ain't no way."

"I don't know. I think we can do it."

And the conversations and arguments continued.

Up on Sweetheart Circle on the campus of Georgia Southern, Dale Lick busied himself in the final days of his administration. The popular president had resigned earlier in the summer to accept a similar position with the University of Maine, and the week of the Florida game was his last in the office he had occupied for seven years.

It was appropriate that Lick's last act as president of Georgia Southern would be attending the Florida game. It was Dale Lick who had started this football program, and it was Dale Lick who told people years earlier that this program would make it to the big-time. There had been skeptics, but now Lick could smile and reflect on the visions he had in the early days. The skeptics were wrong and he was right, and even though winning

the national championship in 1985 may have been the crowning accomplishment, the Florida game was certainly a credit to Dale Lick's dream.

Game week approached and the frenzy continued to build among the Eagle fans. The weekly booster luncheon normally held at the Statesboro Holiday Inn had to be moved to the Williams Center on campus to accommodate the overflow crowd. The luncheons, which occur every week during the season, are usually casual, light-hearted affairs. Everyone comes to hear Erk, expecting some funny jokes and a couple of good stories. There are always the preliminaries. That week, Booster director Frank Hook tidied up a few details on travel and booster plans, and scouting specialist Dr. Pat Spurgeon talked of Florida's greatness. The room, filled with some 250 people, listened intently to each speaker. But when Erk walked to the podium, the frenzy that had been building exploded into pure pandemonium. Normally reserved people stood and cheered. Lawyers, bankers, businessmen for every walk of life were on their feet cheering the man. A giant Eagle flag was waved in the back of the room by a hearty supporter. Whoops and hollers resounded throughout the building. Television camera lights from Savannah and Atlanta flashed in brilliance illuminating Erk. Cheerleaders danced in a corner.

Erk just stood there. Normally he would quiet such a crowd, but there was no hope of doing so this time. The place had gone bonkers, and so Erk just stood and let them cheer.

In a few moments, the room quieted and the people sat, all eyes focused on Erk.

"The Florida game is the most important game we'll play because it is the next one" Erk said. "They are bigger than we are. They are stronger than we are. And they are faster

Chris Aiken (18) knocks down a pass intended for Florida's Ricky Nattiel

than we are. Listen, folks, you look at this game on paper and there just ain't no way. But any time you tee it up, anything can happen."

The crowd believed him. They were all looking for some semblance of confidence from Erk and that one phrase was all it took. Anything can happen.

Erk sensed the excitement and the tension in the room, but he still wanted everyone to realize that this was still just one game out of eleven. He needed to stress that this wasn't a one-game season.

"However," he continued. "If things get out of hand, we'll rely on our motto: Drop back and save the equipment."

The line was the perfect remedy for the tension-filled audience. They broke into laughter and, just for a moment, life in Statesboro was back to normal. Each person breathed a sigh of relief and each leaned back in the seats. Erk had said the right thing again and made everybody relax.

He didn't want to lose all the excitement, though, and his parting words rekindled the fire of frenzy.

"If I die, they can bury me upside down just so Florida can kiss my . . ." — he paused, the crowd anticipating his last word — "my foot."

The crown exploded again, this time laughter mixed with cheers. The cheerleaders screamed, "One more time! One more time! One more time! One more time!"

* * *

109

Georgia Southern practiced on Friday before game day at Florida Field. It was an overcast day, a light rain falling intermittently. Erk was not his usual jovial self. A story, originated by the *Macon Telegraph*, quoted unnamed sources as saying that Georgia Southern's football program was under investigation by the NCAA.

The story appeared in all the papers in Florida, and suddenly, like the thunderstorm that had struck Gainesville earlier in the day, a dark cloud hung over the Georgia Southern program.

"It's a lie," said Erk as he watched his team go through a light workout on the field. "A dirty trick by somebody. This program is clean, and besides, in order for the NCAA to investigate somebody, they must first notify the president of the college, the athletic director and the football coach, and none of us has heard a thing. Why would somebody want to do this to us right now? It's a dirty trick, just a dirty trick. I'd like to know who did this to us."

The sources were never named, and the following day another story appeared saying that the program was not being investigated.

That day, though, the story didn't matter. It was game day. All the hype would end and all the questions would be answered. The dreariness of the wet day in Gainesville didn't dampen the enthusiasm of the 7,200 Georgia Southern fans. They cheered when the Eagles came out for the pre-game warmups, and they could be heard despite sixty-seven thousand Florida fans.

Erk stood on the sidelines watching his team. Tom Stinson of the *Atlanta Constitution* walked over to talk to Erk. Not a normal thing for a coach to do — talk to a reporter just an hour before the game — but, then again, Erk is not normal in terms of college football coaching styles, and he chatted about the atmosphere surrounding the game.

The Florida Gators, dressed in their bright orange jerseys, ran onto to field. The sixty-seven thousand fans cheered wildly and Erk watched them.

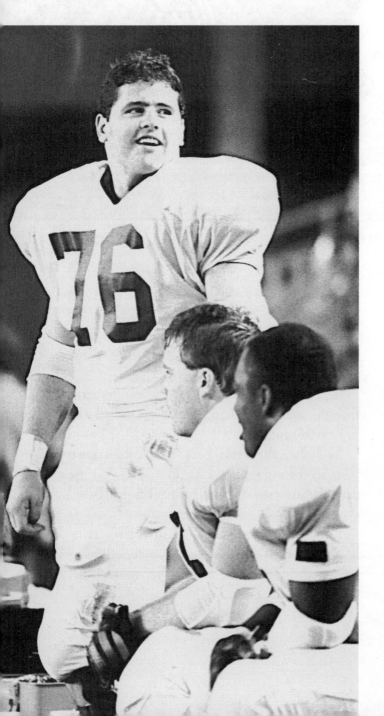

Dennis Franklin (76)—two years and two national championships

"You know, Tom," Erk said to Stinson. "The only way we'll block a Kerwin Bell pass is if he hits one of his linemen in the back of the head." And he wandered out to his troops to prepare them for one of their greatest challenges.

The Eagles were nervous and it showed on the first couple of plays. Wayne Williams split the Georgia Southern defense for eleven yards, then twenty-six on the next carry, and Florida had first and ten at the Eagles fifteen yard line.

On first down Donnie Allen tackled Williams for a one-yard loss, then Chris Aiken batted away a Kerwin Bell pass in the end zone to force a third down situation.

Bell dropped back to pass and Tyrone Huff rushed in untouched, grabbing Bell around the waist. Eagle fans cheered wildly, but inexplicably Bell wriggled loose from Hull, who fell to the ground grasping only a towel. Hull had tackled Bell from behind, and when he reached around the quarterback's waist, he grabbed what he thought was jersey but instead was the towel that Bell keeps tucked in the front of his pants. Bell scampered sixteen yards for a touchdown. Following the extra point, Florida led 7-0. Little did the Eagles know at the time, but that play would symbolize the day, a day of "almost, but not quite."

Four possessions later, early in the second quarter, Chris Aiken again found himself guarding Ricky Nattiel, reputed to be the fastest wide receiver in the South. Twice earlier Nattiel had worked against Aiken, and twice earlier he had come up empty. Aiken had batted away the pass in the end zone in the first Florida drive, and two drives later he had scooped up an errant Bell pass for his first interception of the season.

This time, though, it was Nattiel's turn. Aiken dove but didn't get it. Nattiel did.

Touchdown Florida. 14-0, Gators.

A dejected Chris Aiken sat on the bench holding his hand six inches apart, explaining to his fellow defensive backs how close he came to stopping another Bell aerial.

"I should've had it," he mumbled. "I should've had it." Almost, but not quite.

Out on the field, Gerald Harris fumbled and Florida recovered at its own forty-one yard line. Ten plays later the Gators scored again, and a rout appeared to be in the making. Gators 21-0.

The heralded Georgia Southern Hambone offense had not run more than five plays in succession all day. With 2:33 left, it appeared as though Georgia Southern would be held scoreless in the first half.

Southern fans had quieted and the Florida fans sat smug in their seats smelling victory. Following the kickoff, Ham hit Herman Barron for five yards to the Eagle twenty-nine yard line. Then Ham danced around left end for eleven yards. Another pass to Barron, this one for six yards. Ham around right end for eight yards. Ham around left end for thirteen yards.

The Eagles were in Florida territory. The fans in blue began to cheer. The fans in orange began to shift uneasily. Erk patrolled the sidelines, unable to stand still. Ham completes a pass to Frank Johnson eighteen yards to the Florida nineteen. Gerald Harris ran up the middle for six yards. Ham carried for seven yards to the Florida seven-yard line.

Eagle fans cheered wildly. One thing that Georgia Southern followers learned in the championship season of 1985 was that nothing is impossible as long as Erk Russell walks the sidelines and Tracy Ham takes the snaps. Georgia Southern was moving the ball on Florida. Georgia Southern *could* beat Florida.

Ham rolled left looking into the end zone. Two Florida defenders pursued him. He was in trouble. The sideline was close. The defenders were within arm's reach of him. Ham whirled and threw back to the right, but it wasn't one of his normal passes. This one just floated, wobbly, and Adrian White, clad in the orange of Florida, leapt and caught it.

Tony Belser, the intended receiver, fell to his knees behind White. Almost, but not quite.

Florida built its lead to 31-0 in the third quarter before Georgia Southern could make its mark. Gerald Harris scored on a fourth-and-one situation at the Florida one to cut the lead to 31-7, and then Tim Foley kicked a successful onsides kickoff and five plays later Ham scored from ten yards out to cut the score to 31-14.

But it was too late. Florida scored again to win, 38-14.

The locker room was quiet after Erk said a few words. He didn't tell them that they should have won nor did he dwell on the game itself. He just told them that it was one game, that there were ten more to go and that they needed to work hard the next couple of weeks to get ready for Florida A&M.

Brad Bowen lay on a trainer's table as team physician, Dr. Robert Swint, sewed up a cut on Bowen's chin. It looked painful, the threaded needle weaving in and out, but Bowen didn't seem to notice. A native Floridian, he had wanted badly to beat his home state university, a school that had snubbed him out of high school. His eyes stared at the ceiling as if the reasons for defeat were etched somewhere in the woodwork.

It didn't matter that they had lost to a "big-time" school. It was a loss nonetheless, and the Eagles weren't accustomed to that. It had been ten months since Southern had tasted the bitterness of defeat. It hadn't changed any; that taste was still bad, and it

showed in the unflinching eyes of Brad Bowen. Doc Swint kept sewing.

At the Georgia Southern practice fields the following week, the atmosphere was different. The waters of Beautiful Eagle Creek still sat stagnant, a reminder of a long hot summer that was short on rain. The black gnats swarmed in full force, attracted to the sweat of the boys in white. Erk still shuffled around the fields clad in a time-worn gray T-shirt proclaiming the message "Just One More Time" across his chest and a tattered pair of cut-off baseball pants.

But there was not the herd of reporters who had been watching the Eagles in the pre-Florida days. Nor were there any fans hanging around watching the seemingly dull routine of practice. It was just Erk, the assistant coaches, managers, trainers and the players. This was a work week. Time to right what went wrong against Florida.

Erk often jokes about the Georgia Southern practice fields — "The only practice fields in America surrounded by three major highways." And it's true. On one side is the softball complex, but the other three sides are constantly moving with traffic. U.S. 301 runs past one end, state highway 67 on the opposite side and Zetterower Avenue on the third.

Across the street on the highway 67 side, Wendy's, Burger King, Popeye's and Johnson's Minit Mart do a steady business. Hardee's sits on U.S. 301, and Snooky's Restaurant and the Spee Dee Dry Cleaners dot the Zetterower landscape.

All have their place and connection with Georgia Southern, but none more than Snooky's. It is a nondescript restaurant — a square brick building on the outside, an assortment of booths and tables on the inside. College paraphernalia dots the walls. Composite pictures of sororities and fraternities, a big stuffed fish mounted on one wall, a laminated copy of a *Sports Illustrated* story about Erk on another. At lunch, for $3.50 one can get a choice of meat, three vegetables and a bottomless glass of tea. Snooky's country fried steak is a local favorite, as is the fried chicken, and the banana pudding is as good as anybody's, especially if you happen to be in the restaurant when it comes out of the oven.

Snooky's is the place where locals gather to discuss all the important topics of the time. It was here where football was discussed long before the college began its program, and it is here where several decisions about the program have been made since its inception.

One can sit in Snooky's and look out the big windows across Zetterower Avenue and watch the Eagles practice . . . that is, until the dust stirred up by the constant shuffling of feet obliterates the view.

In the spring of 1986, following the Eagles' first national championship, a group of men sat in Snooky's and watched Southern going through spring drills. The omnipresent cloud of brown dust hung over the field. The men figured that a national champion ought to have better conditions in which to practice, and wheels were set in motion. Wayne Johnson and Joe Smallwood were the ring leaders who spearheaded a campaign to rebuild the two football practice fields and the baseball infield at a cost of $175,000. They enlisted the help of Kenneth Collins, Gene Giddens, John Roger Akins, Johnny Altman, Gary Duncan, Homer Parrish, Donald Nesmith and Ralph Lightsey. Several businesses joined in, including South Georgia Landscaping, Lamar Reddick and Associates, Clay-Ric, Inc., Tifton Turf Farms, Rotary Corporation,

Despite major knee surgery, Robert Underwood anchored the GSU defense

Macon Supply, Hodges-Turner Funeral Homes, Lawn and Turf, Inc., Kennedy Concrete, Southeastern Utilities Contractors, Inc., Statesboro Floor Covering, and Wal-Mart. The Bulloch County Board of Commissioners and the mayor and city council of Statesboro, along with Statesboro Homebuilders Association, joined in, too, and by the time fall practice started in 1986, two resurfaced practice fields were in place and ready to use, as well as a training room and storage area adjacent to the fields.

All because one day a group of men sat in a restaurant and decided something ought to be done for Erk and his boys. Miracles happen at Snooky's restaurant.

113

It was a hot, muggy night at the Gator Bowl in Jacksonville, Florida, as Georgia Southern prepared to meet Florida A&M for the third time in three years. The Eagles entered the game in an unaccustomed position — bearers of a losing record, 0-1. Twice before these two teams had met, and twice before Georgia Southern had won, but both games had been close.

Several assistant coaches lounged on the visitor's bench a couple of hours before game time soaking in the last rays of the September sun. If they were nervous, they didn't show it. Secondary coach Mike Sewak had the choice seat — right next to the huge fan blowing air toward the bench. Florida A&M came out for pre-game warmups dressed in their white jerseys and green pants.

The Eagles assistants eyed them casually, commenting occasionally on the size of one or two of them. There was not much emotion shown by the coaches or the Eagles when they took the field. There was business to take care of — let's do our job, win a ballgame and go home. But Florida A&M had other ideas.

After holding the Rattlers on their first possession, the vaunted Hambone offense, which had struggled against Florida, took the field. Eagle fans knew it was time for the offense to break loose and display the prowess it had shown in the 1985 playoffs. Not this time, though. Three plays and a punt. The Eagles were still struggling.

Again the Eagle defense held and again the Hambone began operating. On the first drive, Georgia Southern had tried two passes, had tried to make something big happen quickly. This time it was different. This time it was business. Frank Johnson gained sixteen yards on the first play and five on the next. Ricky Harris picked up six and Ham gained three.

Nothing fancy, just business. Gerald Harris gained eight and followed that with three. Ham ran for three and then for nine. Gerald gained five and then scored from four yards out. No celebrating though. Tim Foley added the extra point. Eagles, 7-0.

The Rattlers managed two field goals on their next two drives to cut the lead to 7-6. Georgia Southern's offense was still sputtering.

With six minutes left in the half, the Eagles regained possession at their own twenty-two yardline. Three running plays netted fifteen yards. On the next play, Ham hit Johnson for twenty-five yards and Harris gained fifteen more on the next snap — a flash of flash from the Eagle offense. A one-yard gain and an incomplete pass left the Eagles with a third and nine at the Rattler twenty-one. Eagle fans squirmed uneasily in their seats. Where was the excitement? Where was the unpredictability? Where was Tracy Ham? The questions came quickly in their minds. Was 1985 a fluke?

No, answered Tracy. It was time to stop the questioning. You want flash and excitement. Ham darted around right end, slipped two tackles, dodged another, and cut back across the field; a split second after those questions had popped into the minds of the fans, they disappeared without a trace as Ham crossed the goal line, ball thrust into the air in his strong right hand.

At that moment, the electricity of Ham spread through each player as if each were a copper conductor. The defense held. Ricky Harris gained ten. Ham hit Johnson for thirty-three yards. Ham hit him again for twenty. Ham rolled out, connected with Herman Barron for seven, then took the next snap and shot straight up the middle for fifteen yards and another Eagle touchdown. The offense had started clicking, and the race was on for another national championship.

The Eagles added two more touchdowns in the second half. Gerald scored from five yards out and Ham teamed with Tony Belser on a thirty-six yard pass play. Georgia Southern won, 35-12.

Tim Foley had been waiting, sometimes impatiently, for an opportunity to kick a field goal. The Eagles had played two games and all he had done was kick seven extra points. A kicker of Foley's ability wants to do more than that.

There were several reasons that Foley wanted the chance. First of all, he was coming off an All-American year. The Associated Press had called him the best kicker in the country in Division I-AA in 1985. Secondly, he had a streak going. Outside of baseball players, kickers keep up with numbers more than any other type of athlete. Foley had made his last twelve kicks of the 1985 regular season. He needed one more to set a I-AA record for consecutive field goals made. Foley knew it. Erk Russell knew it. Opportunity just hadn't presented itself in 1986.

That Tim Foley even had the opportunity to set a national record was amazing. Coming out of Ocala Forest High School in Ocala, Florida, Foley was considered anything but the best kicker in America. If fact, no school wanted him. He walked on at Georgia Southern because the program was new and he thought he might have a chance to play.

He learned how to kick from a woman named Diane Dodge in Ocala. Her son had kicked at the University of Kansas, and although she couldn't kick herself, she had read a lot on the subject and passed on her knowledge to Tim.

Foley didn't look like a kicker, either. At 5-10, 220 pounds, he looked more like an offensive lineman or a guy who spent most of

Tim Foley set four NCAA Division 1-AA kicking records in 1985 and '86

his time *watching* football games rather than playing in them. During his first week of practice at Georgia Southern, Erk told him he looked like Yogi Bear, and the nickname stuck.

Kicking coach Dr. Pat Spurgeon also thought Foley looked like something other than a kicker. During the first days of practice, Spurgeon told Foley he didn't think he would be able to kick at Georgia Southern and that he would help him transfer to another school which might be interested in his services.

Foley was ruffled by Spurgeon's remarks. He knew he could kick. He just needed the opportunity. So he decided to stay and prove

Spurgeon wrong. And he had.

A few hundred miles up the road in Murfreesboro, Tennessee, Boots Donnelly was preparing his Middle Tennessee State Blue Raiders for what they considered the rematch of the 1985 playoff contest. Twice the Blue Raiders had defeated the Eagles soundly, in 1984 and in early 1985, but Georgia Southern had knocked Middle Tennessee out of the playoff picture in the quarterfinals in 1985, and the Blue Raiders had a score to settle.

In Statesboro, Tim Foley kept kicking in practice, regularly connecting from sixty yards out. Scouts on hand to watch a handful of the seniors took note of the junior kicker, jotting down his name for future reference. Opportunity would knock sooner or later, and Foley wanted to be ready.

Several hundred Georgia Southern fans made the trip to Murfreesboro, some to watch the game and others to relive last year's major upset in the playoffs. The players wandered around the field in pre-game warmups remembering the past, remembering the victory over the Blue Raiders, remembering the Eagle fans chanting, "One More Time! One More Time!"

At the other end of the field the Blue Raiders remembered, too, as did their fans. If there is such a thing as hate in college football, Middle Tennessee State hated Georgia Southern at that moment.

They transformed that hate into a quick touchdown. Just two minutes and nine seconds into the game, Marvin Collier found a wide open Dwight Johnson on a thirty-seven-yard scoring play, and the Blue Raiders were up early, 7-0.

The Eagles tied the score seven minutes later, capping a ninety-yard scoring drive on a six-yard run by Ham. Foley added his eighth extra point of the season to make it 7-7.

The two teams swapped punts for the next twelve minutes as the Blue Raiders found ways to stop the Hambone. At 8:57 of the second quarter, Dwight Stone found the end zone for Middle Tennessee to give the Blue Raiders a 14-7 lead.

The Hambone needed to respond and did. Another ninety-yard drive with Gerald Harris scoring from eleven yards out allowed Foley's extra point to tie the score at 14-14, where it stayed until halftime.

Tim Foley trotted into the locker room at the half clutching his field goal tee in his left hand, still waiting for the opportunity that had yet to arrive.

Inside the locker room, underneath the visitors' stands at Red Floyd Statium, the players huddled with their position coaches watching a maze of X's and O's scattered across the chalkboard. Tim Foley sat in the corner talking with punter Pat Parker, still holding the kicking tee.

Just before the players exited, Erk gathered them around in a big circle.

"We didn't play our best in the first half," he told them. "We need to do better. The offense is going to score in the second half. All we need to do on defense is stop them once and we'll win. Go make yourself proud."

The defense took Erk's words to heart, holding Middle Tennessee on three plays and forcing a punt. The offense had been listening, too.

Starting from his own forty, Ham hit Ricky Harris for eleven yards and then scampered around left end for nineteen more. After a five-yard illegal procedure penalty, Ham threw two incompletions and then hit Monty Sharpe for ten yards, but not enough for the first down.

Tim Foley trotted onto the field. He spotted his tee on the twenty-seven yard line.

Monty Sharpe crouched to hold the snap as Foley marked off his yardage.

"I was really nervous on that kick," he later said. "It had been kind of frustrating not getting to kick, and now my first chance was in a tie ball game. I tried to concentrate on what I was doing. The second I kicked the ball, though, I knew it was good. I could just feel it. I felt like the world had been lifted off of my shoulders. It was quite a relief." Foley had the record, and Southern had the lead.

The defense held again and Ham took the Eagles on another touchdown march, hitting Sharpe on a forty-two-yard scoring pass to give Georgia Southern a 24-14 lead.

Erk had told the defense to hold them once. For good measure, the defense had held twice, giving the Eagles the opportunity to build the ten-point cushion. Middle Tennessee followed the Ham-to-Sharpe touchdown with a score of its own to cut the lead to 24-21.

True to Erk's word, the offense kept clicking. A five-play, twenty-six-yard drive ended on a five-yard touchdown run by Ham. Eagles, 31-21.

But Middle Tennessee kept coming back. Dick Martin kicked a forty-eight-yard field goal to cut the lead to 31-24. No need to worry, though. Erk said the offense would score. They hadn't been stopped in the second half, and on the first two plays of the next drive, nothing seemed different; Ham hit Sharpe for nine yards and then carried for four more himself. But then it happened — Ham fumbled the snap, and Middle Tennessee recovered at the Georgia Southern thirty-five yard line.

Everything had gone according to Erk's plan; the defense had held twice and the offense had been scoring. But Erk hadn't planned on a fumble.

The Blue Raiders wasted no time, as Dwight Stone took the handoff and ran thirty-five yards for a touchdown. The extra point tied the score at thirty-one.

The fumble rattled the Hambone, and on its next possession they could manage only two yards in three plays. Pat Parker punted it away.

Erk huddled his defense on the sidelines.

'The Swainsboro Bush Hog,' Gerald Harris: He'd rather go over than around

"You've got to hold them just one more time," he pleaded.

Stone carried up the middle for eight yards on the first play, and the Blue Raiders were moving again at the Georgia Southern thirty-six. Marvin Collier rolled right second down, looking for a receiver, when all of a sudden the ball popped loose and Flint Matthews pounced on it. No one knew what caused the fumble, but the opportunistic arms of Matthews took advantage of the miscue, and the Eagles had a chance.

The defense danced off the field, arms waving. Erk had told them to hold, and they had. The defense had put the Hambone back in business. After a one-yard gain by Ham, he hit Delano Little for eighteen yards to the Blue Raider forty-five. Gerald Harris got the call on the next two plays, gaining six yards collectively. Ham burst up the middle for twenty-three yards, but the gain was wiped out by a clipping penalty. Gerald Harris gained seventeen on the next play, though, and then pounded up the middle for four.

The clock was now a factor. Less than three minutes remained in the game. Ham pitched to Frank Johnson, but Middle Tennessee swarmed in, causing a five-yard loss back to the fifteen-yard line. Ham then threw an incompletion, causing a fourth-and-eleven situation.

Erk turned to his placekicker. Tim Foley had come into the game looking for an opportunity. He had gotten it when be broke a 14-14 tie earlier. Now he was being asked to do it again. The clock showed 2:03.

"All the relief I had felt after making the first kick disappeared," said Foley. "It was my ball game now, a chance to win it. I could feel the pressure, but just like the first one, the minute I kicked it I knew it was good. I could just feel it."

And he was right. The ball floated through the uprights, giving Georgia Southern a 34-31 lead.

The defense was called on again, and again it held. Georgia Southern was 2-1.

If there was a defense that could master the Hambone, Georgia Southern had not played against it yet. But if there was a defense that could slow the Hambone, it belonged to UT-Chattanooga.

In 1984 and 1985, Georgia Southern had beaten the Mocs, but barely both times. The reason? UT-Chattanooga could contain Tracy Ham. Statistically, Ham had had the worst days of his career against the Mocs. His worst days, of course, would be considered good by some quarterbacks, but by Ham standards they were sub-par.

The Southern defense knew going into the game that the offense probably would not score at will against UT-Chattanooga. The Moc defense was known for its stubborness and its ability to prevent long drives. Georgia Southern's offense would need good field position, and to get it the defense would have to create opportunities.

The Eagle defense had become the whipping boys of Georgia Southern football. Fans marveled at the Hambone offense and the magical ability of its namesake. Tim Foley was as good a kicker as anyone. So when one looked for a problem area, the finger was usually pointed at the defense.

Georgia Southern gave up more than three touchdowns per game on the average, but when the offense was scoring at five touchdown per game, the defensive effort was satisfactory, if not outstanding.

Few people denied, however, that the defense just didn't have as much talent as the offense. Georgia Southern's defense was comprised of a group of undersized over-achievers, a group of guys who gave everything they had each time out but sometimes were simply overmatched in athletic ability. Danny Durham was a perfect example.

Durham was in his fifth year at Georgia Southern and was not anywhere close to being the best athlete on the team. He was small — 5-10, 180 pounds. He was slow,

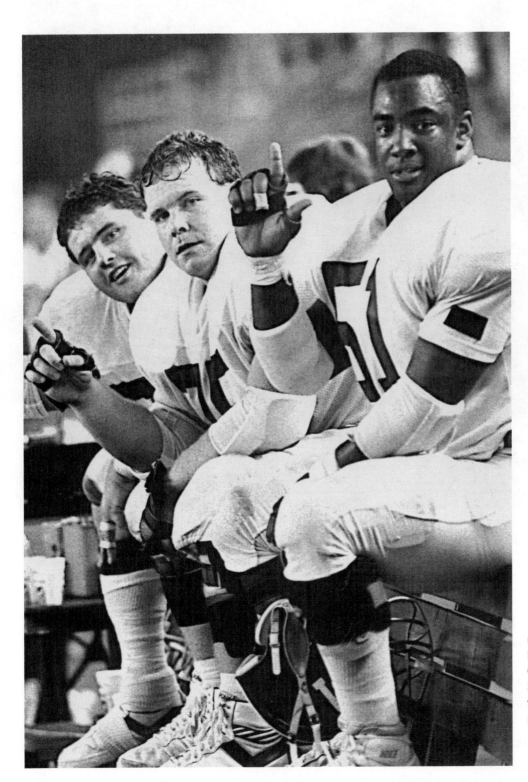

(Left to right):
Dennis Franklin, Charles Cochran and Sean Gainey gave the Hambone offense room to operate

119

Erk gives instructions to Maurice Barron, a dedicated Eagle

especially for a rover, and he didn't possess particularly good hands, usually a necessary quality on pass coverage. But somehow he got the job done every time out.

Danny knew he lacked a lot of ability, but he had two things going for him: He was smart and he wanted to win. Give Erk Russell a player with those two characteristics and championships are the results.

A devoutly religious young man, Durham was not prone to fits of rage on a football field nor was he a cheerleader-type player either. He just played hard. He won the respect of his fellow players, who elected him defensive captain in 1986.

Durham was a symbol of the heart and soul

120

of the Georgia Southern defense. What he — and they — lacked in ability was made up for with desire. And it all could be needed this day.

UT-Chattanooga took the opening kickoff and drove to the twelve-yard line of Georgia Southern before settling for a thirty-yard field goal and an early 3-0 lead.

Georgia Southern responded, capping a thirteen-play, seventy-two-yard drive with a twenty-four-yard Foley field goal to tie the score.

The Mocs drove to the Eagle thirty-nine before their next drive stalled and the two teams swapped punts. The Eagle defense was topping UT-Chattanooga while the offense was searching for the right combination to score on the pesky Moc defense.

The Eagle defense needed to create an opportunity and it did so on the last play of the first quarter when Chris Aiken intercepted an errant Tim Couch pass, giving Georgia Southern the ball at its own forty-six yard line. Ham tried two pitchouts, one to Herman Barron and one to Frank Johnson, but both times the ball was bobbled. On the third down Ham cut up the middle for seven yards, but it wasn't enough. The Eagles had to punt and the opportunity was lost.

Pressure on the much-malinged defense continued to build. The offense was struggling as it had in the past against the Mocs. UTC moved to midfield. Couch dropped back to pass for the third consecutive play, but this time Milton Gore stepped in front of the intended receiver, nabbed the pass and ran it back to the UTC forty-one-yard line. Two plays later, though, Ham fumbled the snap and UT-Chattanooga recovered. The defense had provided two scoring opportunities, but the high-powered, highly-publicized offense had yet to capitalize.

Couch rolled right for UTC, gaining two yards, then tried to dump a pass over the middle. However, Flint Matthews caught it instead of the receiver, and he rambled to the UTC thirty-six-yard line.

For the third time in three drives, the defense had created something. The offense trotted onto the field while the crowd shifted restlessly in the stands.

The Eagles came to the line of scrimmage but without Tracy Ham. Sophomore Ken Burnette took the snap and handed off to Gerald Harris, who gained four yards. Where was Ham? On the sidelines, head trainer Doc Smith worked on the All-American. On the previous drive, Ham had been struck in the groin area and was slow to recover. Burnette huddled the team on second down but before he could call the play, Ham scrambled through the maze of players on the sideline and worked his way toward Erk.

"I'm ready, coach, I'm ready," he shouted, and without stopping he trotted past Erk and onto the field.

The crowd roared. The largest crowd in Paulson Stadium history — 15,234 — cheered wildly. The fans, who had been relatively quiet until now, suddenly found something to ignite them. The familiar No. 8 trotting onto the field provided the impetus.

Ham called the play, then brought his troops to the line. Taking the snap, he rolled right and found Frank Johnson over the middle for a twenty-yard gain. He rolled right again for a gain of two, then rolled left for three more yards. On third down and five, Ham ran a quarterback draw only to be stopped short of a first down by less than a yard at the UTC eight.

Erk called timeout. A field goal was a guarantee from here, but Erk knew the offense needed a confidence builder, and he knew that he needed to get the crowd back in the game.

"Go for it," he told assistant Jay Russell. Up in the coaches' booth offensive coordinator Paul Johnson called the play, relaying it to Jay who in turn gave it to Ham.

Ham handed to Gerald Harris off right tackle for three yards and a first down. The Eagles smelled the end zone now. Harris again went off right tackle. No gain.

On the next play, Ham stuck the ball in Harris' stomach again. But as the defense collapsed toward the middle of the field, Ham pulled the ball away from Harris and trotted around right end untouched for the score. The Eagles led, 10-3.

The fans relaxed. All was once again right with the world. The offense had finally scored.

UTC was thinking different thoughts, however, on the other side of the field. Foley kicked off to Darryl Streeter, who took the ball at the two-yard line and returned it all the way to the Georgia Southern thirty-three.

The relaxed atmosphere in the stands dissipated. The defense had to do it just one more time. The Mocs gained nine yards on the first three plays and faced a fourth-and-one at the Eagle twenty-four-yard line. Brad Patterson, who had replaced Couch at quarterback for UTC, rolled right. The defense pursued, knowing it needed to make yet another big play.

Tyrone Hull shed his blocker and grabbed Patterson around the ankles, bringing him to the ground inches shy of a first down.. The defense ran off the field as the fans on the homeside gave them a standing ovation.

Four times in a row, the defense had stopped the Mocs. Yet, the Eagles had only ten points to show for it. Ham knew it was time to capitalize and put UT-Chattanooga out of the game. He dropped back on first down and lofted a pass to a streaking Frank Johnson. The ball was tipped by a defender, but it proved to be a perfect tip for Johnson, who caught the ball and outran the defense for a seventy-three-yard touchdown play — the longest in school history at the time.

Georgia Southern led, 17-3.

With the offense seemingly back on track, the defense knew its job was done. It was time to have some fun. Brad Bowen intercepted a Patterson pass at the one-yard line on UTC's next drive to end the first half.

The Mocs kicked a field goal on their first possession in the second half to cut the lead to 17-6. But despite the close point margin, the Eagles were filled with confidence. They somehow knew they had the game won.

Georgia Southern drove the ball eighty yards in fourteen plays, with Gerald Harris scoring the touchdown on the ensuing drive. The Eagles led, 24-6.

Thomas Porter intercepted a Couch pass on the next drive, the fifth of the day by the defense, and the game appeared well in hand. Bruce Holbrook and Jerry Ellenburg would also grab interceptions later in the game, and the offense would add another touchdown on a twenty-one-yard run by Ham and three more points on a twenty-four-yard Foley field goal.

The defense had collected a school record seven interceptions in the game. For all the attention the offense had received, this day belonged to the over-achievers. The Eagles had won three in a row and now stood at 3-1.

The first four games of the 1986 season had been a tough run — on the road against Florida in Gainesville, Florida A&M in Jacksonville, Middle Tennessee in Murfreesboro and the lone home game against UT-Chattanooga.

The Eagles needed a breather. An open week would have been nice but the schedule did not allow for it. Instead, Georgia Southern had to travel to play Tennessee Tech in the quaint town of Cookville. That may have been the next best thing.

The Tennessee Tech football program had been in a downward spiral for several years. Former Golden Eagle standout Jim Ragland had been hired prior to the 1986 season to attempt to rebuild the struggling program, but Tech was winless heading into the Georgia Southern game. At last an easy game for the Eagles. Take a nice ride up into the mountains, kick a few butts and come back home with a fourth win.

Erk saw it differently. He knew that Georgia Southern had more talent than Tennessee Tech and he knew that Georgia Southern should win the game, but it was precisely those things that worried him. Overconfidence is something that every coach fears.

Erk preached about it all week.

"This is a team struggling for identity," he told his players. "What better way to establish themselves than to knock off the defending national champions. We've got to go up and *win* that ballgame. They are not going to roll over and play dead just because we're Georgia Southern."

The players listened, or at least tried. But the fans around them talked of a rout. Losing was not even a consideration.

Erk preached to the fans, too. At the weekly booster luncheon, he warned of how a team must take everything one step at a time. There is no looking ahead, no looking past a team. Tennessee Tech was the most important game because it was the next one, and that was as far as he could see.

In typical Erk style, he related a story to the Eagles' situation.

There was a dairy farm, and on this farm there was one bull to service all the cows. The farm kept growing and soon there were too many cows for one bull to handle, so the farmer brought in a younger bull to help out.

His first day on the job, the younger bull was standing with the older bull on a hillside overlooking the valley where all the cows were grazing. The younger bull was anxious, ready to get started.

He turned to the older bull and said, "Why don't we run down there and get us one?"

The older bull smiled and replied, "Why don't we walk down there and get them all?"

Erk had made his point: Take it one step at a time.

Still, however, a certain cockiness existed among the Eagle fans, and when Georgia Southern kicked off to start the game, the small group of fans that had made the trip laughed and joked, enjoying the calm night. As Tennessee Tech threw an incompletion on its first play from scrimmage, the fans seemed more enthralled with a hot air balloon floating up beyond one end zone than they were with the game. After all, this was Tennessee Tech and Georgia Southern should have no trouble with them.

But Tennessee Tech didn't get the message. They kept picking up three yards and four yards per play until finally the Eagles stopped them on third down at the Georgia Southern twenty-four. The Golden Eagles settled for a forty-one-yard field goal and took a 3-0 lead.

Still, no need to worry in the stands. Tracy Ham and company had not taken the field yet, and when they did it would all be over for Tennessee Tech.

Georgia Southern gained eight yards on its first two plays, then Ham ran around right end to gain a first down at his own thirty-yard line. On the ensuing play, however, Ham threw into double coverage and Tennessee Tech intercepted, taking the ball to the Eagle twenty-one.

Six plays later, Tennessee Tech scored and led the defending national champions, 10-0. The unthinkable was coming true. Georgia Southern was running down the hill trying to get 'em all.

Jay Russell gathered his offensive unit on the sidelines. Ham talked on a headset to Paul Johnson in the coaches' booth. Meanwhile, Georgia Southern was penalized on the kickoff, backing the ball up to the Eagle eleven-yard line.

"Let's don't get fancy," Johnson told Ham. "Take it down their throats."

Gerald Harris opened with four up the middle, then four more off tackle left. Steve McCray gained four around left end. Ham turned the corner on the left side and gained fifteen yards, then ran a quarterback draw for ten more. The Eagles had moved to their own forty-eight-yard line.

Georgia Southern pounded out three yards on the next two plays. On third-and-seven at the Tech forty-nine, Ham hit Monty Sharpe for fifteen yards to the thirty-four. Harris then broke off right guard for a thirty-two-yard gain down to the two-yard line, and two plays later he scored Georgia Southern's first touchdown. The Eagles trailed, 10-7. It stayed that way for the rest of the first quarter.

The Eagles settled for a twenty-yard Foley field goal early in the second quarter to tie the score at 10-10. After holding Tech on its next drive, the Hambone cranked up again, traveling eighty-three yards in nine plays with Gerald Harris scoring from one yard out to give Georgia Southern the lead 17-10. Four minutes later, Ham scored on a three-yard keeper, expanding the lead to fourteen points. Tech added a field goal just before the half to cut the lead to 24-13 at intermission.

The Eagles led by eleven points, but it wasn't what everyone had expected. No rout

was taking place. Tech was playing it close. Erk gathered his troops in the lockerroom.

"There is no tomorrow, men. Let's go back out there and do what we came to do. Don't let up and don't quit."

Georgia Southern took the words to heart.

The Eagles did not allow another point in the second half, while on the offensive side of the ball Georgia Southern experienced its greatest half of football. The Eagles scored thirty-five second-half points. Gerald Harris scored on a seven-yard run and McCray scored from twenty-three yards out. Ross Worsham caught a forty-yard pass from Ken Burnette and Taz Dixon returned an interception fifty-five yards. Third-string quarterback Ken Bullock capped the scoring with a four-yard run.

Georgia Southern had started the game running down the hill chasing just one of Erk's mythical cows. They finished the game walking, ready to get 'em all. Georgia Southern won, 59-13, and the Eagles stood at 4-1.

Georgia Southern was reputed to have the best offense in Division I-AA. No team knew that better than the Wildcats of Bethune-Cookman. In two previous meetings, the two teams had combined for 146 points and more than 1,700 yards in total offense. 1986 would prove to be no different.

The Eagles were fresh off a fifty-nine-point performance against Tennessee Tech and seemingly had the offense clicking in its highest gear. Georgia Southern had the ability to score a lot of points in a short period of time. The Hambone struck quickly and without warning. Boom. Boom. And the scoreboard would light up, the Georgia Southern side changing as fast as in a basketball game, while the other team stood on the sidelines amazed at the smoothness and

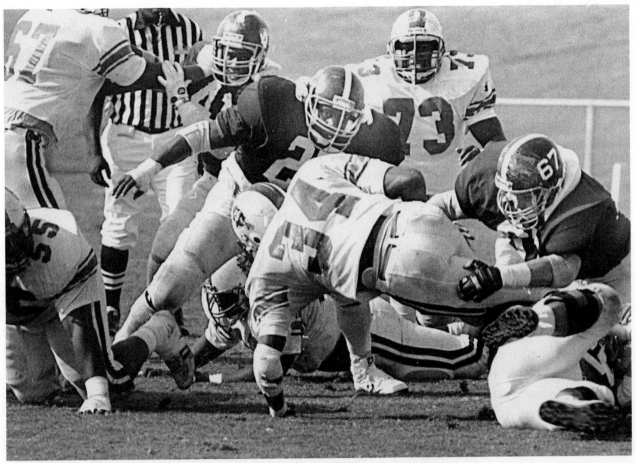

Charlie Waller (67) and Kenny Butler (20) close in on a Bethune-Cookman runner

quickness with which touchdowns were scored.

The Hambone was a strange offense, but it was growing in popularity throughout the country. Following the 1985 season, coaches from other schools flocked to Statesboro to learn the intricacies of it. Offensive coordinator Paul Johnson explained it to them.

To a person not familiar with the language of football, listening to his explanation sounded like a strange linguistic mixture of half-words and numbers: 370 wheel. Three technique scoop. Blue over. A hodgepodge of phrases.

To the football layman, Johnson explained the offense this way:

"It's sort of like wishbone," said Johnson, "except we take the two halfbacks and instead of lining them up next to the fullback, we put them in slots on each side of the line. What we've done is taken a passing formation out of the run-and-shoot offense and made it into a running offense. It seems to give defenses trouble because it's not an offense they see every week."

The Hambone was capable of sustaining a fifteen-play drive to consume time on the clock or to score at a moment's notice when points were needed quickly.

Bethune-Cookman had received a couple of lessons in the 1984 and 1985 meetings. In 1986, they would get their final course.

The Wildcats scored first on a twenty-seven-yard field goal to take an early 3-0 lead, which they held through the first quarter. Meanwhile, the Wildcat defense seemed to come up with the big play at the right time to thwart the Hambone for the first fifteen minutes. But whatever they did right in the first quarter disappeared in the next thirty minutes.

In the second and third quarters, the Hambone posted fifty-two points on the board, thirty-one of them coming in the second quarter alone. Ham scored on a twelve-yard run, capping a nine-play drive in which the Eagles had ground it out. Gerald Harris scored on the Eagles next two possessions — once on an eleven-yard run and once on a five-yarder.

Less than two minutes later, Georgia Southern regained possession and took only one play to score again. Ham rolled right, spotted Tony Belser streaking down the sideline, and hit him with the pass. Belser outran the defense, going seventy-seven yards for the score and breaking a two-game-old record for the longest play in Georgia Southern history. Tim Foley added a forty-yard field goal just before halftime, giving the Eagles a 31-10 lead.

In a space of fifteen minutes, Georgia Southern had left the Bethune-Cookman defense bewildered, confused and twisted by the whirlwind of the Hambone offense.

Whatever semblance of order that was left in the Wildcat defense disappeared in the first minute of the second half. On the third play from scrimmage, Ham ran a quarterback sneak, a play that is designed to gain a couple of yards at best — a couple of yards for everybody except Ham. He shot straight through the middle of the defense untouched for fifty-five yards and another Georgia Southern touchdown.

Ricky Harris scored on a twenty-four-yard touchdown later in the quarter, and Garry Miller added a twenty-two-yard touchdown run toward the end of the third to seal Beth-une-Cookman's fate.

The Wildcats scored a couple of consolation touchdowns in the fourth quarter, but the Hambone had overwhelmed them again. Georgia Southern had won its fifth game in a row, 52-21, and now had a date with East Carolina.

This was an unusual position for the Georgia Southern Eagles. In two previous tries against I-A opponents, the Eagles had fallen short, losing to East Carolina, 34-27, in 1984 and to Florida, 38-14, in the 1986 season opener. In both games, the Eagles were heavy underdogs — in 1984 because they were an unknown quantity in college football circles and in 1986 because Florida was expected to be a serious contender for the Southeastern Conference championship.

Their third try against a I-A opponent was coming up — another shot at East Carolina, whose program had gone from 8-3 in 1983 to one of the worst in the division in 1985. An NCAA investigation and the firing of head coach Ed Emory had left the once-powerful Pirates in shambles, and new head coach Art Baker was trying to revive a moribund team.

The position for Georgia Southern was unusual because the Eagles had been picked by almost everyone to win the game. Rarely is a I-AA school picked to topple a bigger school, but Georgia Southern had earned the respect of the oddsmakers and East Carolina had fallen out of favor to the point where the Eagles were a nine-point favorite.

Erk didn't like being picked to win. He loved being the underdog. He thrived on it, relished it.

"I can't figure how they can pick us to win," he said that week. "They're having a bad year, but any way you look at it, they're still a I-A school with forty more scholarship players than we have. They've got more players and more quality athletes."

Still, the oddsmakers predicted a Georgia Southern win.

The Eagles were hurting on offense, too. Starting guard James "Peanut" Carter was sidelined with a calf injury, and Ronald Warnock, normally a guard, would have to start at tackle because Tony Smith was also hobbling. The offense line was patchworked together with very little depth.

That Ronald Warnock was even playing college football was amazing. Guys like him usually have great high-school careers but don't advance any further. In the Southern program, Warnock was listed as 5-11, 240 pounds. In reality, he was 5-9, 215 pounds with his pads on. The typical offensive tackle in college stands 6-4 and weighs 250-plus pounds. But somehow, Warnock survived.

"You can take a guy who is 6-5, 275, and say he is going to be a good one," said Erk. "But the one thing you can't measure about a player is how bad he wants to win. Warnock wants to win, and he has to want to win pretty bad to play with his size."

Against East Carolina, Warnock lined up opposite David Plum, who stood 6-3 and tipped the scales at 252 pounds. He had Warnock outsized by six inches and thirty-seven pounds.

By the end of the day, the entire Southern team would feel puny.

Two years earlier when the Eagles had played in Greenville, a crowd of more than twenty thousand had awed them, causing a loss of composure. East Carolina had capitalized on that and jumped to a 21-0 lead before the rowdy fans in the student section could mix their first drinks.

On this day in 1986, though, the Eagles were not bothered by the 27,121 folks in the stands. Just five weeks earlier, they had played before more than seventy-four thousand against Florida, so the East Carolina crowd had become relatively small in comparison.

Georgia Southern did not want to fall behind early again — they wanted to take control of the game, dominate it and win it. Don't get behind. Don't give a team on a

James Carter (96) was the only true freshman to play in 1986

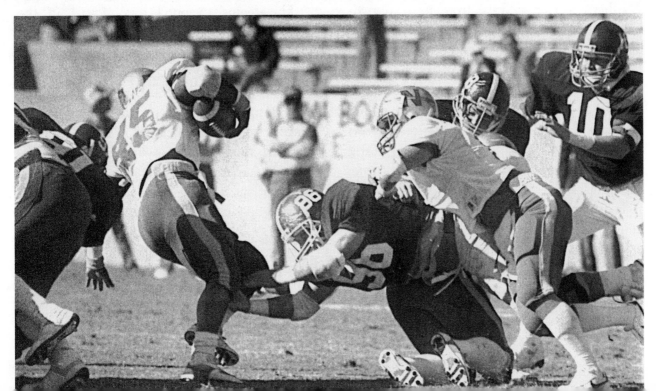

downslide any sense of hope. That was the game plan.

It didn't work out that way.

The Pirates took the opening kick and drove seventy-six yards in sixteen plays and then converted a two-point attempt to take an 8-0 lead. On Georgia Southern's first possession, Frank Johnson fumbled the ball away and East Carolina drove sixty-one yards in ten plays to jump ahead 15-0.

The gameplan was falling apart. The Pirates had jumped ahead early. They now had hope. They now tasted their first victory of the season.

On the other side of the field, Georgia Southern did not panic. They didn't like being behind, 15-0, especially this early, but they had been behind before.

Gerald Harris went straight up the middle for thirty-seven yards on the Eagles' first play of the next drive. Ham followed with a scrambling eleven yards to the East Carolina twenty-five. Four plays later, Ricky Harris scored from eleven yards out, and Gerald ran the two-point conversion to cut the score to 15-8.

At the start of the second quarter, Georgia Southern started a drive from its own two-yard line. Ninety-eight yards lay between the Eagles and a tied ballgame.

Ham up the middle for six. Ham up the middle for six more. Ham to Belser for twenty-one. Ham off right end for eight. Ham up the middle for four. Ham to Johnson for twenty-one. Georgia Southern was piling up the yardage. Harris for four. Ham for thirteen. Ham for six.

Fourteen plays after the Eagles stared at ninety-eight yards of open field, Ham carried it in from one yard out. Foley's extra point evened the score at 15-15.

Now the confidence and taste of victory changed sidelines. Georgia Southern's chests swelled and East Carolina was reeling. Again.

The ensuing kick changed everything, though. Anthony Simpson returned the kick to the Eagle thirty-four, and seven plays later Chuck Berleth kicked a thirty-eight-yard field goal to give the Pirates a 18-15 lead.

After swapping punts, Georgia Southern took possession at its own eighteen-yard line with two minutes remaining in the half. For most teams, two minutes is a time to run a drill to move the ball up the field quickly. Not much time, gotta move quick. But for Georgia Southern, two minutes is an eternity. The Eagles had proved through the first five games that they could score as quickly and easily from seventy-five yards away as they could from five.

Ham scrambled for twenty-one. Johnson gained five and East Carolina was penalized fifteen for a personal foul. Ham hit Johnson for thirty-six yards. After an incompletion, Ham found Belser for nineteen yards and then ran the ball for one on the next play.

Less than ten seconds remained. Foley sprinted onto the field. The snap. The kick from thirty-two yards out. Good. The horn blew and the game was tied, 18-18.

The teams swapped touchdowns in the third quarter, leaving the score 25-25 with fifteen minutes to play. East Carolina felt it was fifteen minutes away from its first win of the season. Georgia Southern felt it was fifteen minutes away from proving the oddsmakers right and knocking off a I-A team for the first time.

East Carolina drove the ball sixty yards in twelve plays to forge ahead, 32-25. Still 9:03 showed on the clock. Plenty of time for Tracy Ham.

He mixed his plays brilliantly. A couple of runs and a quick pass. A couple of more runs, another pass. Georgia Southern marched down the field. And the clock ticked.

With 2:59 remaining, Ham scampered across the goal line from three yards out, and Georgia Southern trailed by one point, 32-31.

There was no doubt in Erk's mind what to do. No team goes into a game looking to lose and no team goes into a game looking to tie. Erk's teams look to win.

Erk relayed the play to Ham. Ham took the snap, faked a handoff to Gerald Harris, bounced off one tackler, spun away from another and drove, stretching his muscular body toward the goal line. To the fans in the stands, Ham's body seemed suspended in air for several minutes. All eyes focused on No. 8.

He hit the ground with a thud, the ball in the end zone. The referee thrust his arms into the air and Georgia Southern led, 33-32. The Eagles were less than three minutes away from their fifth straight victory. The sideline was jubilant. It was party time in Greenville. Even though the oddsmakers had predicted a Georgia Southern win, a victory over a I-A school, regardless of talent, regardless of record, would be yet another milestone in the rapid growth of the Eagles' fledgling football program.

Foley kicked off to Anthony Simpson, who returned it well to the East Carolina forty-four-yard line. Two-and-a-half minutes remained. Georgia Southern's defense dug in. Simpson gained six up the middle to midfield, then Travis Moody was stopped by Larry Boone for no gain. Third down and four to go. If the Eagles could just stop them here. . . . Travis Hunter rolled right and found an open receiver at the Eagle forty-three. First down, East Carolina.

Simpson gained five to the thirty-eight. The clock ticked. Simpson gained another yard. Boone tracked down Hunter on the next play, stopping him after a three-yard gain. It was fourth down at the Georgia

Southern thirty-four-yard line. Just more than a minute remained. One yard separated the Eagles from the ecstasy of their fifth straight victory and first over a Division I-A team and the gut-wrenching possibility of losing yet another close one to East Carolina.

Hunter handed off to Simpson off right guard. He slipped through the hands of one tackler before Donnie Allen could wrestle him to the ground. And when the ball was spotted, Simpson had stretched his body for five yards. First down, East Carolina, at the Georgia Southern twenty-nine.

Forty seconds remained. Hunter, under a heavy rush, threw incomplete. Second down. Hunter rolled right, but underthrew the receiver. Third down. Hunter dumped a pass to Simpson on the right wing, but Robert Underwood read it perfectly and dropped the fullback for a one-yard loss at the thirty-yard line.

Twenty seconds remained. East Carolina was out of timeouts. The Pirate field goal unit sprinted onto the field. Kicker Chuck Berleth quickly marked off his steps. He looked up. Forty-seven yards lay between him and the goalpost. The snap was perfect. The holder placed the ball on the tee. Berleth swung through it, lofting the ball above the outstretched hands of the Eagle defenders. It floated, end-over-end, and for a moment that seemed like eternity, a sliver of time, there was not a noise to be heard in Ficklen Stadium. A slight wind ruffled the hair of the spectators and the collar of Erk's shirt. Art Baker stood on the Pirate sideline, his fists clenched at his waist, lips pursed in a moment of ultimate intensity.

The ball began its descent. The closer it got to the goal post, the more uncertain the outcome became. The East Carolina fans broke the momentary silence, as if hoping their cheering would somehow push the ball through the uprights. The Eagle players and fans yelled, too. From silence to pandemonium in a matter of seconds. The ball came downward headed straight for the crossbar.

But the breeze that had ruffled Erk's collar seemed to reach the crossbar at the precise instant as the ball. Aided by that breeze, the ball cleared the bar by a matter of inches — three at the most.

The Pirate fans danced in the stands. Art Baker leaped into the air. Chuck Berleth was mobbed by his teammates. On a lonelier part of the field, Tyrone Hull sank to his knees, his head dropping toward his chest. The sun reflected off the number 87 on his chest and the grass stains on his white pants. He threw back his head, looking into the sky and seeing nothing but a picture-perfect patch of Carolina blue.

He slowly rose from his kneeling position and trotted off the field, never looking at the scoreboard that read: East Carolina 35, Georgia Southern 33.

With a week off following the loss to East Carolina, the Eagles had time to think. They remembered that in 1984 they posted a record of 8-3 and didn't make the playoffs, and they remembered that in 1985 they finished the season at 9-2 and received an at-large invitation to the tournament.

Georgia Southern currently stood at 5-2. In the players' minds, one loss could mean elimination from playoff consideration and a lost opportunity to defend their national championship.

The eighteen seniors on the team met on Monday after the East Carolina game and talked about the situation.

"We told the whole team that we had to win the rest of them," said Tracy Ham. "We

didn't want to take any chances at 8-3. We wanted to be 9-2. If we made the playoffs, we wanted to earn it. We didn't want to sneak in the back door. Plus, at 9-2 we had a better chance of hosting a playoff game in Statesboro than we would at 8-3. It was time to put it together and win a few ballgames."

Western Kentucky didn't realize what lay ahead. In the papers in Bowling Green, they talked about Georgia Southern being overrated and how Tracy Ham "looked like he was selfish with the ball."

Ham didn't like that. One thing Tracy Ham was not was selfish. He ran the ball a lot and passed the ball a lot because that's what he thought it would take to win a ballgame. So, in addition to the players feeling like their backs were against the wall, Ham had a score to settle with the Hilltoppers.

The Georgia Southern sports information office had been promoting him as the best quarterback in America. Not in Division I-AA, but in America. No apologies to Vinny Testaverde. No apologies to Chris Miller, Kelly Stouffer or John Payne. Ham was the best, pure and simple.

The Western Kentucky media scoffed at the idea. How could the best quarterback in America be at Georgia Southern? If he was that good, why wasn't he playing at Georgia or Oklahoma or Miami? In a roundabout sort of way, the media was saying "Prove it. Prove you are the best."

Ham did. Six minutes into the game, he made perhaps the most impressive run of his fabled career.

He called an option to the left side of the field. It was first and ten at the Western Kentucky forty-five. Ham came to the line, barked the signals and took the snap. But something went wrong. Ten offensive players went left according to the play. One went right. That was Ham.

When Ham got to the corner of the line on the right side, he realized his mistake. He had no blockers in front of him, but instead seven red-jerseyed Hilltoppers stared him in the face. Ham didn't panic, though. He worked his magic, weaving in and out of the seven players, breaking five tackles along the way, and scampered forty-five yards for a touchdown.

In the press box, the Western Kentucky media gasped.

"Jesus, how did he do that?" said one reporter.

Another just leaned back in his chair and said, "Damn."

Ernie Reese of the *Atlanta Constitution* just smiled. He had been covering Ham and Georgia Southern for three years. He had seen Ham pull off miracle after miracle and nothing surprised him anymore. He would watch Ham turn a nothing play into a work of art, and he would just smile. Ernie had been a quarterback in college a few years back and had a great appreciation for what Ham could do on a football field. In three years of covering him, Ernie Reese smiled a lot.

By the time the halftime horn had sounded, Georgia Southern had built a 35-14 lead, and Ham had carried the ball twenty times for 105 yards and three touchdowns, had completed twelve of twenty passes for 206 yards and one touchdown.

Georgia Southern eventually won the game, 49-35, though the final score made the game sound closer than it actually as. Ham didn't even finish the third quarter. He left the final twenty minutes to Ken Burnette and Ken Bullock.

In the post-game interview room, Western Kentucky head coach Dave Roberts stood at the podium with a tired look on his face. When asked about Ham, he, like Ernie Reese, smiled.

"I have never seen a better quarterback than Tracy Ham. That guy is amazing. Erk has done a great job with that program. That's where I want Western Kentucky football to be — where Georgia Southern is right now."

Real estate agents in Orlando, Florida, get used to strange things. Florida, being a state comprised heavily of transplants from other parts of the country, presents them with the opportunity to meet a vast range of personalities ranging from the normal to bizarre.

Erk Russell would give them yet another story to add to their collection.

The Eagles arrived in Orlando late Friday afternoon scheduled to play Central Florida in the Citrus Bowl on Saturday night. They couldn't practice at the stadium because a high-school game was being played there that night, so Erk had to improvise.

The Eagles were lodged in a Days Inn. Next door was a real estate office, and behind that was a lake. Between the real estate office and the lake was a large, grassy knoll. Erk gathered the team on that spot and started practicing.

In the real estate office, a group gathered at a back window to watch what was going on. They saw seventy fellows dressed in gray sweatsuits and blue football helmets doing calisthenics in their backyard with this bulky, bald-headed guy watching them.

Curiosity got the best of one of them, who finally walked out of the office and toward the bald-headed guy.

"What's going on here?" he asked.

"Football practice," Erk replied.

"Oh," said the man who trekked back to the office with a puzzled look on his face. Just another day at the office.

The Eagles were in for war on the field Saturday night. The two schools had started football at about the same time, but Georgia Southern had progressed in stature light years beyond Central Florida, which was still struggling at the Division II level.

Central Florida desperately wanted a win over the Eagles, and at the end of the first half the game was tied 14-14. Georgia Southern had had two touchdowns called back in the first half on penalties, and yellow flags dotted the field every time the Eagles had a big play. Something was rotten in Orlando and Bucky Wagner knew it. He wasn't sure if the officials were purposely making bad calls to hinder Georgia Southern or if they just were not good officials, but he felt like something ought to be said.

He couldn't reach the Central Florida athletic director because Gene McDowell was also their head football coach, so he cornered another athletic department official.

"I don't know what's going on here," Bucky muttered, "but it better stop. You tell McDowell that if things don't change, this series is over."

Whether the message ever got to McDowell is unknown, but Georgia Southern was able to forge a ten-point lead in the second half, and with thirty-one seconds remaining in the game, the Eagles had the ball on the Central Florida forty-five-yard line, third down and six yards to go.

In the coaches' booth upstairs, Paul Johnson had been watching this Eagle drive and noticed that no one was covering Tony Belser from his wide receiver position. Johnson knew the Eagles could run out the clock, but he wanted to put another touchdown on the board. He told Jay Russell, who was on the other end of the headset on the sideline, to ask Erk if he could call "370 Wheel," which was a straight fly pattern in which Ham threw to Belser.

Jay asked Erk, who said, "Go for it." What Erk meant was to go for the first down. The Eagles were six yards away from it and could run two plays to get it. However, Jay interpreted it differently and relayed the message to Paul.

"Go for it" — Jay gave the play to Ham with a series of hand signals from the sidelines.

Ham dropped back and hit a wide-open, streaking Belser at the five-yard line. Belser trotted into the end zone, no Central Florida defender in sight.

Erk was confused by what had happened.

Gerald Harris (35) set four playoff records in 1986—most touchdowns in a game, most touchdowns in a series, most points in a game, and most points in a series

Jay explained it to him.

"We need to communicate better," Erk said as he trotted off the field, the Eagles seventh victory of the season firmly in hand.

Revenge is not a motive often used by Georgia Southern because, quite frankly, a team that doesn't lose very often seldom has to avenge anything. But in the case of James Madison, revenge was high on the Eagles' priority list.

The Dukes were the last I-AA team to defeat Georgia Southern, having outscored them 21-6 on a miserable, rainy day in Virginia in 1985. Tracy Ham had been injured in the first quarter of that game and had to watch helplessly from the sidelines as the Eagles went down to a rare defeat.

Ham was healthy heading into the 1986 contest in the friendly confines of Allen E. Paulson Stadium. James Madison would find out just how healthy.

The game, played before the largest Paulson Stadium crown ever of 16,135 patrons, was an offensive showdown as expected. The two teams scored seemingly at will in the first half, with the Dukes taking a 24-21 halftime edge.

Ham had a good first half — thirty-eight yards rushing and one touchdown, six-of-eleven passing for 136 yards and another touchdown — but he was saving his best for the last thirty minutes. On the opening drive of the second half, Georgia Southern started at their own twenty-three-yard line, scoring a scant five plays later on a fifty-yard pass from Ham to Monty Shapre. Of the seventy-seven yards covered on the drive, Ham accounted for all but eight of them with his running and passing.

On the ensuing Dukes drive, Brad Bowen recovered an errant pitchout at the Georgia Southern twelve-yard line, giving the Hambone another opportunity. Thirteen plays and eighty-eight yards later, the Eagles scored again with Ham going in from two yards out. Ham gained fifty-five of those eighty-eight yards rushing.

Not to be outdone, James Madison scored quickly on the next drive, taking just three plays. The score set up by an eighty-one-yard kickoff return by Rodney Stockett. Georgia Southern led 35-32.

The Eagles fumbled away the kick, and the Dukes drove down to the Southern seventeen before James Carter knocked the ball loose and recovered. Six plays later Ham had them in the end zone again, this time gaining sixty-one of the eighty-three yards himself.

On the day, Ham rushed eighteen times for 121 yards and three touchdowns and completed twelve of eighteen passes for 258 yards and two touchdowns. In the second half alone, he gained eighty-three yards rushing and passed for 122 more to lead Georgia Southern to a 45-35 win.

James Madison had not seen much of Ham in 1985. In 1986, they saw more than they wanted to. Revenge was sweet, and Tracy Ham enjoyed the taste.

Georgia Southern entered the South Carolina State game at 8-2, one win shy of clinching a playoff berth and the right to defend their 1985 national championship.

Ham had played three great games in a row. He was due for an off day, and he had one against South Carolina State. He rushed for only twenty-seven yards on sixteen carries and completed only one of eight pass attempts. But the mark of a championship football team is its ability to take up the slack when the star is not playing up to his potential. In this case, a November Saturday belonged to Gerald Harris.

Erk Russell referred to Gerald as the "Swainsboro Bush Hog": "He runs low to the ground and knocks down everything that gets in his way."

When South Carolina State got in his way, he ran them over with ease. When the day had ended, Harris had accumulated 169 yards rushing on just sixteen carries and had scored one touchdown.

Georgia Southern had won the game, 28-7, and had earned a spot in the playoffs.

In 1985 the playoffs were a mystery of sorts to Georgia Southern. As the new kids on the block, they were tasting the do-or-die emotion of a national championship drive for the first time. In 1986 they were the old pros, the team everybody wanted a piece of.

An old sports axiom says "If you want to be the best, you have to beat the best: Georgia Southern was a marked team.

Eighty-eight teams started the season in Division I-AA. The field was now down to sixteen and only one could wear the national championship crown. No team had ever won back-to-back national championship in I-AA, and no team had done it in Division I since Alabama captured titles in 1977 and 1978.

Four games lay between the Eagles and college football history. The cards had been dealt and destiny was now ready to play her hand.

15 | *A 'Zone' Defense Works To Perfection*

Jackson State had come to Statesboro in 1985 to play the Georgia Southern Eagles in the opening round of the playoffs. They had brought with them an air of supremacy and cockiness and had even resorted to feeble attempts at verbal intimidation during the Friday night banquet honoring both teams.

Their ploy had not worked as Georgia Southern had whipped them, 27-0, vaulting the Eagles into the quarterfinals.

The opponent in the opening round of the 1986 playoffs was North Carolina A&T, a school known for producing outstanding basketball teams but a relative unknown in I-AA football circles.

On Friday afternoon before the game, a small press conference was held at the Lupton Facilities Building at Allen E. Paulson Stadium. North Carolina A&T head coach Mo Forte brought his top two players with him — quarterback Alan Hooker and defensive tackle Ernest Riddick. Georgia Southern countered with Tracy Ham, Gerald Harris and Danny Durham. If the Eagles were expecting the Aggies to act in the same manner as Jackson State did a year earlier, they were in for a pleasant surprise.

The Aggies were not cocky or arrogant. They were nice people. Coach Forte talked of his respect for Georgia Southern's football program and, following the press conference, Ham and Hooker talked informally at length about the different aspects of their respective offenses. It was a friendly gathering, a sense of mutual respect permeating the tension that playoff football arouses.

Erk Russell couldn't waste the opportunity to insert his brand of down-home humor into it. When asked about North Carolina A&T and their outstanding quarterback, Erk replied, "It is the only time in my coaching career that I've given my players permission to chase a Hooker." Mo Forte laughed as hard as anybody.

This was a pure example of what college athletics should be. Two teams preparing for a football game, both wanting to win badly. But off the field, the two teams were just people getting to know each other and making a few new friends along the way.

Whatever friendships formed in the pre-game ceremonies on Friday were not evident on Saturday. The two teams were ready to do what they had come here for — play football.

On its first drive, North Carolina fumbled the ball away to the Eagles at the Aggie thirty-three-yard line. Ham completed a pass to Herman Barron for seventeen yards on the first play, and on first and ten at the seventeen-yard line Gerald Harris exploded up the middle for a touchdown, giving Georgia Southern a 7-0 lead.

It was just one of many touchdowns that Harris had scored in his career. Entering the game, the senior from Swainsboro had crossed the goal line sixty-one times in a Georgia Southern uniform. His first touchdown against North Carolina A&T was just a harbinger of things to come in the 1986 play-offs for Harris.

Eight minutes later, Harris scored from seven yards out, then Ham scored on a nineteen-yard run on the first play of the second quarter to give Georgia Southern a 21-0 lead. The rout was on.

Harris scored his third touchdown of the afternoon on a nine-yard run only seconds after Ham had scored. Tim Foley added a thirty-six-yard field goal, and Georgia Southern sat comfortably ahead, 31-0, at halftime.

The two teams swapped points in the second half, each scoring twenty-one. But the Aggies had dug themselves into a huge hole in the first half, one from which they could never surface. Final score: Georgia Southern 52, North Carolina A&T 21.

The day was more than just a win for Gerald Harris. It was a day of records and a day to remember. He had carried the ball eighteen times on the afternoon and gained 181 yards, a personal high. In the process, he had scored five touchdowns — a Georgia Southern school record and an NCAA I-AA playoff record. In the last two games, Harris had gained 350 yards rushing and had scored seven touchdowns. Not a bad day's work for the "Swainsboro Bush Hog."

While Harris was setting playoff records, the telephones in the press box rang incessantly. Seven other playoff games were in progress, and the eight host institutions (Georgia Southern and the other seven) were busy exchanging scores. The Eagles were slated to play the winner between Appalachian State and Nicholls State in Statesboro the following Saturday. With each score update, members of the media speculated on who would do what in the second round. Appalachian State was a heavy favorite against Nicholls State. The boys from Boone, North Carolina, had been picked in the preseason by *Sports Illustrated* to win the I-AA national title, but when the final horn sounded, the upstart Colonels from the bayou of Louisiana had upset the highly favored home team.

Nicholls State was on its way to Statesboro for a showdown with the defending national champion.

Erk Russell had given permission to his team to chase a Hooker against North Carolina A&T. The Eagles had caught him. Nicholls State brought to Statesboro a rifle-armed senior named Doug Hudson who had led them to ten victories in twelve tries during the season.

Erk didn't waste the opportunity. "Last week we got us a Hooker. Now it's time to dam the Hudson."

Georgia Southern fans were anticipating an offensive shootout at Allen E. Paulson Stadium in round two of the playoffs. Georgia Southern was fresh out of its mistake-free fifty-two-point effort against North Carolina A&T, and Nicholls State, a pass-oriented team, had put a few points on the board throughout the season as well.

On their first possession, the Eagles moved the ball to their own forty-five-yard line where they faced a fourth-and-one situation. With only three minutes gone in the game, it

Opposite: Tyrone Hull (87) made it a long afternoon for North Carolina A&T quarterback Alan Hooker

136

was a normal situation in which to punt. The score was tied 0-0. But, then again, Erk does not always make normal decisions.

"Go for it," he yelled to Jay Russell, who got the play from Paul Johnson in the booth and signaled it to Ham on the field.

On the previous play, Gerald Harris had plunged into the line and had come up empty. The Nicholls State defense was expecting the same thing this time. Ham approached, checked the defense, and although he didn't show it on his face, he was smiling inside.

"I knew when I looked at the defense that the play wouldn't work," Ham said in a post-game interview. "They were ripe for a surprise."

Surprise may not have been the proper word. Shock might have been better.

Ham took the snap and faked the handoff to Harris. When that happened, all eleven defensive men charged to the middle of the big pileup. Ham snatched the ball out of Harris' stomach, tucked it under his right arm and darted around right end, not a defender within five yards of him.

Ten seconds and fifty-five yards later, Ham tossed the ball to an official in the end zone, and the Colonels stood on the sideline trying to figure out what had happened.

Erk knew he was taking a big gamble and knew he would have been second-guessed for a long time had the play not worked, but he chose to chance it anyway.

"I figured, Why mess around? I wanted to find out just what kind of game we were in for. That situation was as good an opportunity as any to answer that question."

The shock of the play threw Nicholls State completely out of balance, and before they could recover, Georgia Southern had scored twenty-eight unanswered points. Following the Ham run, Gerald Harris scored from one yard out on the next drive to make it 14-0.

Four minutes later, he scored on a four-yard run, and on the second play of the second quarter, Ham hit Tony Belser with an eleven-yard scoring pass to make it 28-0.

The two teams swapped points for the rest of the game, but the lightning-quick strike from the Hambone in the first quarter had put the game out of reach early. Final score: Georgia Southern 55, Nicholls State 31.

On the other side of the country, Tennessee State was no match for the nation's top-ranked I-AA team, the Wolfpack of Nevada-Reno. UNR rolled to its thirteenth win of the season without a defeat.

The Wolfpack wanted to play Georgia Southern. They wanted to be the ones to knock off the defending national champions and they knew they would. Said one Nevada-Reno player after the win over Tennessee State, "If that's what football in the South is like, we will have no problems with Georgia Southern." A heady statement for a team that had lost in the semifinals of the playoffs in four different years and had yet to make it to a national championship game. A statement, too, that made it back to Statesboro quickly and into the ears of one Erk Russell.

There are certain things a team should not do when preparing to play Georgia Southern, but the most unforgivable sin of all is to talk about how good you are and how Georgia Southern will be no problem. Erk thrives on those types of situations. Give him an underdog team and he'll produce a winner. Give him an opportunity and he'll take advantage of it. Give him a statement like the one made by the Nevada-Reno player and he'll motivate his team to its highest level.

Erk's assistant coaches and players never downgrade the opposing team, regardless of their quality. Tennessee Tech is as tough as Florida in Erk's eyes, because it is the next game. Nevada-Reno is the toughest because it is the next game.

"Anytime you tee it up," Erk often is quoted as saying, "anything can happen." The Wolfpack of Nevada-Reno should have listened to the silence coming out of Statesboro and interpreted it accordingly. Instead, the coaches, players and fans were making plans for the national championship game the following week in Tacoma, Washington, and no one in Reno, Nevada, gave Georgia Southern a second thought. Just another game, just another win.

Wake up, Reno, the Eagles are coming.

Erk wasn't sure he liked the idea of taking this team to Reno, Nevada. The vast majority of the players had never been to a city quite like this one — twenty-four hours a day, casinos on every corner, pleasures for sale that most of the guys had only read about in the magazines that were sold from behind the counter at the local convenience store.

The 1986 Georgia Southern Eagles were a strange bunch anyway. Put them in Reno, Nevada, and its anybody's guess what might happen. Erk called this team "goofy."

"I can't figure them out," he told a reporter earlier in the season. "But somehow they get ready to play on Saturday, and I guess that's the bottom line."

Assistant coach John Pate was amazed at this squad, too.

Pate was a military man, used to orderly things, and a self-confessed sports junkie. He had come to Georgia Southern in 1985 after serving as head coach of Union College in Kentucky for one year. He had an image of what it took to win a national championship.

"This team has destroyed the myth of what I thought a national champion was like," said Pate. "You have this image of a group of guys working hard, serious-minded, dedicated to one thing and one thing only — and that's winning. These guys, though, they work hard and they want to win, but they are so

Assistant coach Jimmy DeLoach plots strategy against Nevada-Reno

relaxed. Nothing bothers them. They're just so loose."

It was not unusual on any given practice day to stand around and talk to the players who were not involved in what was going on at that exact moment and listen to them talk about the girls they met last night or what they were planning to have for dinner that night. When they weren't directly involved in what was going on on the field, football

139

seemed to be the last thing they wanted to talk about. Somehow, though, when it was time for those players to participate in practice, they would step in and everything would glide as smoothly as if they had been listening intently to every word and carefully eyeing every move that had been made.

Erk was right — this team was "goofy."

The folks at Nevada-Reno knew that playing in their home city could work to their advantage. Since most visiting teams had never been there, they were usually awestruck at the glitter and light. The Nevada-Reno people suggested that the team stay at a place called The Nugget, a hotel-casino as plush as any in the city.

Erk knew better. The longer he kept the players away from the casinos, the better off they would be. He told Nevada-Reno, "Thanks, but no thanks. We'll stay at the Holiday Inn."

Erk arrived at the Holiday Inn, his portfolio in one hand, the initials ER sewn in script on the side, and in the other hand a milk jug of brown, brackish water with a piece of tape on the side. Handwritten with a black felt pen on the tape were the words, "Beautiful Eagle Creek Water." It was his jug of magic, and the players would occasionally gaze at it as if it were a golden idol or a national championship trophy.

The hour was late when the team arrived and Erk sent them off to bed. They had a big day on Friday — practice at the stadium and a host of reporters who wanted to talk to them. The media wanted to know about this team from South Georgia, the team that everybody in Reno knew would lose to the mighty Wolfpack.

Friday morning's *Reno Gazette* brought more inflammatory comments from the Navada-Reno players, and the television newscasts on Friday night were the same. Georgia Southern was being set up as a sacri-

ficial lamb on Reno's march to a national title.

Television crews and newspaper reporters were out in full force on Friday. They came to see Georgia Southern run a few plays and to watch the Ham kid operate at quarterback. What they saw instead was a group of fifty-two players in matching gray sweats and blue helmets running all over the field playing pickup games of tag football. Tracy Ham was not at quarterback, he was playing wide receiver. Tackle Fred Stokes was calling the signals, and on one play he tossed a spiral for a touchdown to Mike Wagner who narrowly eluded the outstretched hand of center Dennis Franklin who that day was playing cornerback.

One reporter saw Stokes throw and whispered to a colleague, "I didn't realize Ham was that big." Stokes is 6-4, 260 pounds. Someone else corrected him and pointed to Ham toward the center of the field.

The reporters in Reno, like the ones everywhere else the Eagles had visited, were mystified by the jug of water that Erk carried around the field with him. Cameras zoomed in on the jug as reporters mentally prepared their stories for that night's newscast about the strange bald-headed fellow with the jug of dirty water.

Forty-five minutes after the Eagles had trotted onto the field, Erk gathered them in one end zone. He turned to the sports information director and asked him to make sure the cameras didn't film what was about to happen.

Erk unscrewed the top from the jug, bringing cheers from the fifty-two players. The group, surrounding Erk like a pack of bodyguards, walked slowly down the middle of the field sprinkling drops of the magic liquid from one end zone to the other. The Reno observers watched, giggling at this unorthodox pre-game ritual.

They interviewed Erk about the ritual afterwards and they talked to Tracy, too.

"Word has it that there had been a big rush on luncheon meat at the grocery stores," one reporter told Ham.

"Why's that?" asked the quarterback.

"Supposedly, the zonies are going to throw the stuff at you when you come on the field."

"Seems like a waste of good food to me," said Ham, smiling.

"They can be intimidating," responded the reporter.

Ham grunted in agreement.

The zonies were a group of fans — students mostly, but a few townspeople thrown in — who sat in one end zone of the stadium and verbally intimidated the opposition, in this case, Georgia Southern. They were rowdy, unruly and unpredictable, occasionally throwing objects on the field at the opponents and showering them with beer and other consumables. They were the talk of Reno. No way Georgia Southern could operate in front of that kind of crowd. Or so they thought.

What the zonies didn't know was that Georgia Southern refused to be intimidated.

Attempts to rile them only made them play better. If the zonies thought Nevada-Reno football was the best in the country, they were in for a big surprise on Saturday.

A crowd of more than fifteen thousand jammed into Mickey Stadium to watch the game. The Eagles took the opening kick at their own thirty-six-yard line and drove to the Reno seven in thirteen plays. Ham couldn't convert on a third-and-one situation and Tim Foley was called on to boot a twenty-four-yard field goal, giving the Eagles a 3-0 lead.

The crowd cheered wildly when the Reno offense took the field. The Wolfpack offense had not found a defense yet that could stop them, and they showed little respect for the Eagle eleven who had been giving up twenty-five points a game.

On first down, however, Robert Underwood batted down a pass attempt by Eric Beavers. Reno gained six on the next play, but on third down Flint Matthews blitzed and sacked Beavers for a nine yard loss. Three downs and a punt. The fans were silent.

Georgia Southern started its next drive at

The 'Zonies' tried to intimidate the Eagles, but to no avail

its own forty-seven. They netted only three yards on the first two plays and a third-and-seven situation at midfield. The fans were happy; Reno was going to hold the Eagles. Ham didn't agree, as he rolled around right end and gained thirteen yards for a first down. He then hit Tony Belser for thirteen more to the Reno twenty-four.

Beyond the twenty-four yards on the field and the ten in the end zone, the zonies were cranking up their noise. For the Eagles to score, they would have to drive the ball into the jaws of the raucous group.

Ham gained one off right tackle, then went around left end for four more. On third down, he again rounded the left side, gaining six and giving the Eagles a first-and-ten at the Reno thirteen. Ham dropped back to pass, then tucked the ball under his right arm and sprinted straight up the middle untouched for a Georgia Southern touchdown. As he crossed the goal line, he looked into the zonies and smiled. He didn't say anything. He just smiled. There was a message in that flash of teeth. The Eagles led, 10-0.

The defense again held and Georgia Southern took over at its own nine-yard line. Ham had the Wolfpack nervous. On the previous drive, he had carried the ball on five of six plays. It was a perfect time for the option.

Ham rolled right and pitched to Ricky Harris, who sidestepped two defenders and raced down the sidelines for fifty-seven yards before he was finally tackled from behind at the Reno thirty-four-yard line. A penalty and an incomplete pass stalled the Eagles, and Foley attempted a fifty-yard field goal. It just missed to the left of the upright and the Wolfpack had escaped first-half humiliation. Or so they thought.

Opposite: Ham scores a sweet touchdown against Nevada-Reno

The defense held one more time, and the Eagles drove eighty yards in just seven plays with the capper coming on a diving catch by Delano Little in the corner of the end zone. Georgia Southern led, 17-0.

The two teams then swapped touchdowns, with Reno scoring on a seven-yard pass and Ham responding with a twenty-two-yard toss to Belser at the other end of the field. The Wolfpack added a field goal on the last play of the first half, and the Eagles trotted to the locker room, past the dumbfounded zonies, with a 24-10 lead.

Five minutes into the second half, Georgia Southern had built its lead to 34-10. On its first possession, Foley had kicked a forty-yard field goal, and then after Edward Eaves recovered a Reno fumble at the Wolfpack forty-yard line, Gerald Harris scored from sixteen yards out and Foley kicked the point after.

The handful of Georgia Southern fans who had made the cross-country trek sat happily in their seats while the zonies grumbled in the end zone.

The Wolfpack added a touchdown at the 6:27 mark of the third quarter, cutting Georgia Southern's lead to 34-17. Still, nothing to worry about in the Eagle crowd. It was still a seventeen-point game.

The Eagles began driving, but Ricky Harris fumbled it away at the Reno thirty-three, and nine plays later the Wolfpack scored again to make it 34-24. Georgia Southern started marching again and in six plays had moved from its own forty-five-yard line to the Reno twenty-two. Another touchdown march was in the making, but Gerald Harris fumbled on first down and the Wolfpack had been given yet another opportunity. Three plays netted twenty-seven yards for Reno, and the crowd was sensing a dramatic comeback. The Georgia Southern fans squirmed uneasily.

143

Above: Ham and Jay Marshall (53) celebrate against the Wolfpack; Opposite: Tim Foley boots another field goal

Almost one year earlier, the Southern fans had been in a similar position. Trailing Furman, 28-6, in the 1985 title game, the faithful had all but given up hope of winning. But then Tracy Ham led the Eagles to that remarkable comeback, to a 44-42 win, while the Furman fans sat in disbelief wondering what had happened.

The Georgia Southern fans were beginning to feel much like the Furman fans must have felt in Tacoma in 1985. A comfortable lead early in the second half, no reason to worry, and then, all of a sudden, the opponent starts coming back and the team seems to be self-destructing.

First and ten at the Reno forty-five, Eric Beavers dropped back to pass. A touchdown would make it a three-point game. Beavers spotted a receiver and fired over the middle. Linebacker Flint Matthews stretched high in the air, his taped and bloodied fingers strain-

ing into the Nevada sky. At the apex of his leap, his hand met the ball, popping it straight up into the air. Rover Danny Durham snagged the ball before it hit the ground and rambled thirty-yards to the Reno twenty-six-yard line.

Durham leaped in jubilation. He was mobbed by his teammates as he came to the sidelines. Whatever kindred spirit Georgia Southern fans had felt with the Furman fans of 1985 quickly disappeared. The Eagles drove. Gerald for five, Ricky for six. Ham for one, then, after a holding penalty, Gerald straight up the middle for twenty.

The Eagles had a first and goal at the Reno four. Ham gained three of them up the middle, then handed off to Gerald Harris for the last one and another Georgia Southern touchdown. Foley kicked the extra point and the Eagles led, 41-24. It was again a seventeen-point game and again the Eagle fans felt content.

Georgia Southern scored once more, on a one-yard run by Ham, and Reno added two more touchdowns and one two-point conversion, but the interception by Durham and the subsequent Harris touchdown had broken the back of the undefeated Wolfpack.

When the horn sounded, the Georgia Southern Eagles trotted toward the locker-room, not celebrating in stereotypical fashion but walking off the field as if they had won just another game. In the end zone, the zonies, heads bowed and eyes blurred, stumbled out of the stands still unsure of what had happened. Reno had lost, and they didn't want to face it.

Kicker Rob Whitton spotted a young boy holding a blue-and-white headband with the word "Zonies" printed on it.

"I'll give you a dollar for that headband," Rob told the kid.

"You can have it," the youngster said. "I don't want it anymore."

144

Erk gets a victory ride following the win over Nevada-Reno

In the locker room, he told his troops to go and do it just one more time

Whitton wrapped it around his head, proudly displaying his souvenir in the Eagle locker room.

In the pressbox upstairs, Tony Stastny of *Savannah Morning News* worked on his column. On his ride to the stadium that morning, Tony had had the unpleasant experience of riding with a particularly obnoxious cab driver. In addition to babbling on and on about how good Reno was, he had taken Tony on an unusual, lengthy and costly ride to Mackey Stadium.

"No way this team from Georgia can win," the cabbie told Tony with a touch of arrogance in his voice. "We got a damn *team*."

At the moment the game ended, Tony Stastny would have paid any fare to ride back to the hotel with that guy. The *team* had been defeated, 48-38, and the cab driver would have to watch the national championship on ESPN.

Georgia Southern versus Arkansas State. The field of sixteen was down to two.

147

16

Same Song, Second Verse: 'Just One More Time!'

GSC assistant coach Pat Spurgeon couldn't believe what he was hearing. In preparing the Eagles for upcoming games, Spurgeon admitted that Arkansas State was the one team Southern should be worried about. This was even before the Eagles upset Nevada-Reno. Reno might have been ranked No. 1 and Arkansas State No. 2, but that wasn't the way Spurgeon saw it. He knew the Indians could play defense and he knew, like Southern, they hit hard.

But from what Spurgeon was hearing the day of the championship game, the Indians didn't have the same respect for Southern that the GSC coaches had in preparing for Arkansas State. The best line, or worst line, was uttered by an ASU assistant in a television interview. He said the Indians had seen two or three better quarterbacks than Tracy Ham during the 1986 season.

Apparently he had been hallucinating.

Though the Eagles had been to the Tacoma Dome for the 1985 national championship, the magnitude of the game and the wait for it to start was gnawing on the coaches, normally a nervous lot anyway. Russell, as usual before a game, seemed distracted. Though only 4,419 were in attendance, the game was on television back in South Georgia and was being carried nationwide by ESPN.

But the players didn't seem to be bothered by the late start or the importance of the game. A day earlier, while Arkansas State ran plays in practice, the Eagles played touch football and sprinkled their cherished "Beautiful Eagle Creek Water" in the end zones to keep ASU out and Southern in.

It wasn't as if the Eagles had ice water in their veins. Jello was more like it. They weren't bothered as much by pressure because they failed to acknowledge it.

Well, not everybody.

Before the contest, place kicker Tim Foley had gone through his usual warm-up routine, beginning with stretching, then kicking field goals from progressively longer distances. It was part of his psych job on himself and the other team. Booting a sixty-seven-yarder in practice, like he did the week before while warming up against Nevada-Reno, can unsettle the opposition. But this time it was Foley who was slightly rattled.

He had shown himself to be human a year earlier when the Eagles pulled off their greatest miracle to beat Furman 44-42 for the 1985 I-AA title. After going through his entire sophomore season without missing a field goal or extra point, Foley missed a twenty-seven-yard field goal while the Eagles fell behind by twenty-two points early against the Paladins.

He could have been a goat, but the Eagles came back with the aid of Foley's three field goals and won the game on a thirteen-yard pass with ten seconds left from Ham to Frankie Johnson, a walk-on freshman at the time.

Still, there was some doubt about what Foley would do in a big game.

As the game began, Arkansas State also appeared to have a case of the jitters. On the Indians' second play from scrimmage, fullback Richard Kimble took a handoff from quarterback Dwane Brown and left it on the Tacoma Dome carpet. GSC senior defensive guard Donnie Allen pounced on the ball at the Arkansas State thirty-five.

"My eyes got real big when I saw that ball just sitting there," Allen said. "Nobody hit him. He just dropped it."

Southern's first series stalled when Ham was tackled on third down at the ASU two-yard line by Indian middle linebacker Dan Miller. Foley rushed onto the field for a twenty-yard field goal attempt. He had more than the usual pressure to think about. His regular holder, Monty Sharpe, was nursing a pulled hamstring, so punter Pat Parker would be holding instead.

"I put the tee down," Foley said. "I looked up at the goal posts and started to think about what I was going to do. When I looked back down again, the tee wasn't there."

"He started looking all over," Parker said. "He finally yelled, 'Pat! Where's the tee? Where's the tee?'"

Parker just shook his head and pointed to his hand, where the tee had been all along. "I told Tim he had to relax."

The kick was good and Southern had a 3-0 lead.

All season long, Georgia Southern's defense had been taking more shots off the field than on it. While the Eagles' offense was setting all kinds of school records for scoring and rushing yardage, Southern's defense gave up its share of points, 25.8 per game to be exact.

Erk Russell, who had made a name for himself by running Georgia's "bend but don't break" defense for seventeen seasons, was taking more than his share of kidding for the Eagles' brand of offensive-oriented football. The funny thing was, Southern's defense had the same style as Georgia's did under Russell, only the Eagles bent a little more and could afford to.

But now they had been insulted. Instead of letting sleeping Eagles lie, Arkansas State quarterback Dwane Brown had popped off in the Tacoma press and television interviews about how he was as good as Tracy Ham and how he didn't see that scoring on Georgia Southern would be much problem.

Brown didn't know how fed up the Eagles' defenders were with that kind of talk. They had heard it all season. Led by leading tackler Robert Underwood, a 5-10, 215-pound junior linebacker, sophomore linebacker Tryone Hull and the strongest man on the team, senior defensive guard Larry Boone, Southern began hitting hard and tackling in droves.

GSC didn't allow a first down or a score until ASU's third drive, when the Indians went ninety-seven yards and capped the drive with a fifteen-yard touchdown off a pitchout from Brown to Boris Whiteside.

After that lapse, the Eagles' defense held ASU's offense scoreless until 5:36 remained in the third quarter — time enough for Southern to take a commanding lead.

It was amazing how little respect the Eagles had gotten. Here was a team that was the defending I-AA national champion but still managed to come in as the underdog in its semifinal and final game of the season. GSC was ranked first in the NCAA's I-AA pre-season poll, but after the opening loss to Florida it never saw the top spot again. At the end of the season, the Eagles were ranked No. 4 and ASU No. 2 to top-ranked Nevada-Reno. Going into the championship game, the Eagles were 11½-point underdogs.

"I don't foresee them coming in and scoring a lot of points," Miller had said before the game. "We've been pretty strong on defense this year, especially when teams get inside the twenty. It goes back to the point of scoring. If you can't score, you can't win."

Little did Miller know he'd be talking about his own team. In Southern's next possession after Foley's field goal, Ham went to work. He ran for thirteen yards up the middle, then ten through a hole in the left side of the line. He passed to Belser for sixteen yards. A seven-yard gain by Gerald Harris put the Eagles at the ASU sixteen, in the area of the field Miller said the Indians could control.

Well, pull the stakes out of the tepees.

Ricky Harris went around left end for seven, and Gerald Harris took over from there with a three-yard run and a one-yard plunge for the score.

After Whiteside's touchdown, Foley hit field goals of thirty and twenty-five yards. On the opposite sideline, ASU head coach Larry

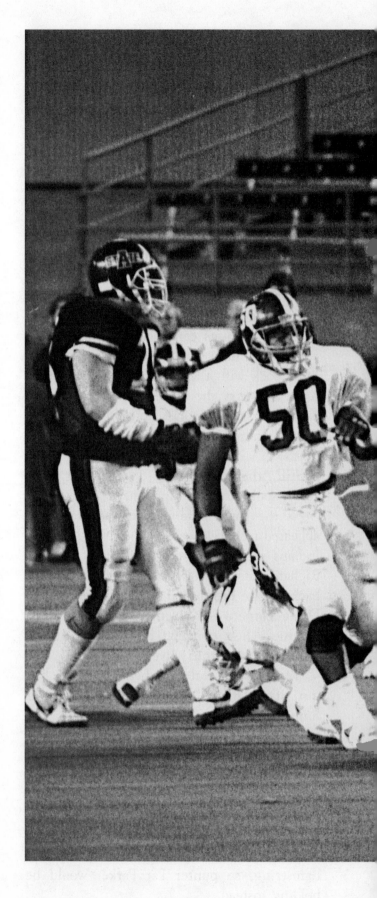

150

Against Arkansas State, the defense played perhaps its best game of the year; Robert Underwood (34), Larry Boone (50) and Tyrone Hull (87) show enthusiasm

Lacewell was pacing. Ham connected for a twenty-seven-yard pass to Ricky Harris on third down from his own nine-yard line. Delano Little dove to catch a nineteen-yard pass on the right sideline. A nine-yard run by Ham brought another first down at the ASU thirty-two. Two plays later the Eagles were faced with a third-down-and-three situation. No problem. Ham rolled slightly to his right before seeing an opening big enough for a twenty-five-yard touchdown. With a Foley point-after, the Eagles led 23-7 midway through the second quarter, and the Indians were reeling.

After Ham was hit with a penalty for throwing an illegal forward pass, Foley connected on another field goal, this time from thirty-six yards, with eight seconds left in the half. Now Lacewell's worry began to show in his players. With time running out in the half, returner Earl Easley tried to pick the ball up but kicked it instead, and it skidded out of bounds. The Indians welcomed halftime.

Ham came out on the first series of the third quarter and led his team steadily downfield. A pass to Ross Worsham for nineteen. Ham scrambles, then fires to Herman Barron for seventeen. Gerald Harris rumbles up the middle for six to the ASU thirty-one. Ham rolls out right to pass again, fakes a throw at the line of scrimmage and finds a seam worth running for — touchdown. Ham then passes to Barron for a two-point conversion. On the sideline, the players start laughing. Russell even manages a smile.

Then, finally, an Eagle mistake. After GSC held again on defense, Southern's drive stalled at its own seven. Parker got set to punt, but Stan Stipe's long snap sailed over

his head, and all Parker could do was watch as the ball went out of the end zone for a safety.

Like the defense, Parker was another one who'd often been maligned. More often than not, however, he was the one doing the maligning. A product of Benedictine Military School in Savannah, Parker took up kicking

Donnie Allen (61) closes in on Arkansas State's Dwane Brown

late in high school. He had been an 190-pound offensive lineman, and the summer before his senior year he was looking forward to starting.

Early that summer, however, he was at a party that got a little wild. Someone picked Parker up and threw him into the swimming pool into about six feet of water. As Parker pushed himself up from the bottom, another person jumped in and landed on Parker's head, snapping it forward. Parker didn't think anything about it at the time, but when he awoke the next morning, he couldn't move the right side of his body.

When he went to the doctor, Parker learned he had a severely pinched nerve and

Gerald Harris rambles for more yardage in pursuit of a national title

was lucky not to be permanently paralyzed. As it was, he was told to give up football or risk paralysis. Parker saw various physicians around Savannah, most of whom told him not to play football.

Crushed, Parker decided to talk to Benedictine football coach Jim Walsh, who told Parker he could kick if he could get himself on his feet again. Parker had fooled around as a kicker and punter but had never tried out for the position.

Parker finally found a physician that would give him the go-ahead, but the doctor cautioned there was a risk of paralysis, though small, if he participated in any contact. Parker had to wear an uncomfortable neck brace for six weeks. Three weeks after the injury, he could move his right arm but had no strength in it. He couldn't throw or catch a

football. But slowly, Parker improved. By the third week of the season, Walsh felt he was ready to punt.

The game was against Bradwell Institute in Hinesville. When Parker went out on the field to punt, Benedictine fans began to cheer. It took Parker a while to realize they were rooting for him. Parker's punt, a high spiral, traveled forty-six yards, but he outkicked his coverage. The punt returner broke a few tackles and pretty soon had clear sailing to the end zone — except for Parker.

His mother, worried for her son, was tempted to run on the field to stop Parker from making the tackle and risking injury. She didn't get there in time, and Parker made the tackle. When he ran off the field, he was chewed out by Benedictine team physician Dr. Paul Jurgensen, but Parker felt fine and knew then things would be O.K. He punted twenty-three times that season averaging over forty yards per kick.

Parker had even tried to be a placekicker for the Cadets, but that didn't work out as well as his punting. In Benedictine's homecoming game against Brunswick, Walsh gave Parker a chance to kick a forty-two-yard field goal just before halftime. His attempt missed badly, going out of bounds. But Brunswick fumbled on its first possession, allowing Parker to try another field goal of forty yards. This kick was short. As the Cadets ran off the field for halftime, thinking time had expired, one of the Brunswick players picked the ball up and ran it back for a controversial touchdown.

Once he got to Georgia Southern, Parker was strictly a punter. Groves High football coach Tommy Brennan, then an assistant at Benedictine, had tried to interest Southern Miss, his alma mater, in Parker, but they weren't interested. The best Parker could get was encouragement to walk-on at GSC. After three seasons, he was still a walk-on. He was consistent, if not spectacular. Except on the ensuing free kick.

A poor kick following a safety and consequent good field position could have sparked the Indians. But in this crucial situation, Parker boomed it sixty-five yards.

Being down twenty-five points, the Indians scrapped their wishbone attack and began to pass. After Brown threw an incomplete pass out of bounds and found Whiteside for a one-yard reception, GSC safety Milton Gore took a gamble, stepped in front of Brown's next pass and intercepted it.

At halftime, receiver Monty Sharpe had confided how disappointed he was about being injured. A pulled hamstring had been bothering him for weeks, and it really began to bother him early against Arkansas State forcing him to the sidelines. He said he knew

Gerald Harris and Tracy Ham celebrate first touchdown against Arkansas State

it was a team game, but as a senior he'd like to be in there anyway. Somehow, by the third quarter, he'd talked the GSC coaches into letting him back in the game. Even with only one good leg, he was the team's best deep threat.

On the first play after Gore's interception, Ham lobbed a ball to Shapre down the left sideline. Obviously limping after the reception Sharpe was knocked out of bounds by the Indians but not until he'd gained thirty-nine yards to the ASU eleven. From there, Ham took a step back, then ran forward through a maze of Indian defenders. Somehow, he came out alone on the other side for another touchdown. It was 41-9, and some of the crowd began leaving, even though 8:17

remained in the third quarter.

Arkansas State finally broke its scoring drought with a fifteen-yard pitch from Brown to Whiteside at the end of the third quarter. But it was too little, too late.

Ham would stay in for two more plays. After Gerald Harris was stopped for a one-yard loss, Ham threw a lob pass over the middle to Ricky Harris, his roommate at GSC. It had been a rough season for Harris, who was the Eagles' leading rusher the year before. He had had to split playing time during the regular season with Johnson, who missed the championship game with a broken ankle. But this time both Harris and Ham would go out in style. Harris caught the pass over the middle in full stride and didn't stop until he'd scored a seventy-nine-yard touchdown. It was the longest pass play in Georgia Southern history and the last play as collegians for Ham and Harris. "If Ricky had dropped that pass, I'd have called him up every year at this time to remind him," Ham said. "If he'd been caught from behind, I'd call him up and remind him of that every year, too."

ASU got one more score in, a forty-four-yard pitch from Brown to Cazzy Francis but only five minutes remained. An onside kick by ASU failed. After a GSC drive, the Eagles held the Indians once more on fourth down at Southern's twenty-five with 1:04 left. All substitute GSC quarterback Ken Burnette had to do was hold onto the ball.

But as the Eagles were running out the clock, there was another game play going on. Ham began to engage Russell in a conversation on the sideline. Meanwhile, senior cornerback Chris Aiken sneaked up from behind with a cooler full of ice water and poured it onto Russell's very bald head.

Fortunately for Russell, Spurgeon was there to hand him a dry sweatshirt. Across the

Despite being 3,000 miles from home, Southern fans made their presence known

156

Erk Russell, Tracy Ham and the Eagles accept the 1986 national championship trophy

front were the words, "Georgia Southern — National Champions '85-'86."

They had done what no Division I-AA team had ever done before.

In the locker room after the game, the seniors danced "The Funky Monkey." Whatever that was, it was obvious they were having a good time. The Eagles relied on teamwork, even when it came to celebration.

Forty minutes later, the late hour and the miles of travel began to subdue the atmosphere. The year before, when Southern won its first national championship with a 44-42 win over Furman, bedlam resulted. That had been a miracle. This time around, even though the Eagles were the underdogs again, there was pride in knowing they'd proved the first time wasn't a fluke. The post-game meal of fried chicken and soda tasted like caviar

and champagne.

From the Tacoma Dome, the Eagles went straight to their chartered plane and began the long flight back to Georgia. Some partied on the way back; most tried to sleep. When they landed at Savannah at 11:30 the next morning, they walked through the Butler Aviation Hangar and were greeted on the other side by an impromptu pep rally. "Holy moley," Russell said.

By 1 P.M., the team had made the bus trip back to Statesboro, where another crowd awaited them at GSC's Hanner Fieldhouse.

"We're tired, we're wrinkled, and I need a haircut," Russell told the group. "But we're No. 1!"

On the sideline, with their second consecutive national title in hand, Georgia Southern players had dumped a cooler filled with ice water on Erk Russell's head. Then each of the eighteen seniors had rubbed his bald dome.

Normally, Erk adamantly refuses to let anyone touch his head. It is just something he doesn't like. But on that night, as the game clock ticked down, he let them. They rubbed and rubbed and rubbed. And Erk Russell smiled.

His dreams had come to fruition. His team, his program, his tradition were all basking in the glow of a second national championship.

Erk has had the Midas touch since coming to Georgia Southern. One day before accepting the job, he said it looked like the Eagles

needed a place to play. Allen E. Paulson Stadium was constructed. He also said that if you surround yourself with good people, good things will happen to you. All the assistant coaches and players who have passed through the doors have been good people. And he has always said that the harder he works, the luckier he gets. Erk works hard. The result is two national championship.

As you read and reread this book, remember it all — the wins and the losses, the happiness and the tears, the good times and the bad times. In years to come, people will look back at the 1985 and 1986 teams and smile, knowing that not once, but twice, Georgia Southern College in the small town of Statesboro, Georgia, was the best in the country. And no matter what happens, that can never be taken away.

And when you remember these times, you will be able to relive them, experiencing the glory of it all JUST ONE MORE TIME!